I0005126

# TABLE OF CONTENTS

**Hackers & Crackers**
Cyber-Criminals Have YOU Targeted!
©Copyright 2013 by Dr. Treat Preston

## DISCLAIMER AND TERMS OF USE AGREEMENT:

**(Please Read This Before Using This Book)**

ideas contained in this book, you are taking full responsibility for your actions.

The authors and publisher disclaim any warranties (express or implied), merchantability, or fitness for any particular purpose. The author and publisher shall in no event be held liable to any party for any direct, indirect, punitive, special, incidental or other consequential damages arising directly or indirectly from any use of this material, which is provided "as is", and without warranties. As always, the advice of a competent legal, tax, accounting, medical or other professional should be sought where applicable.

The authors and publisher do not warrant the performance, effectiveness or applicability of any sites listed or linked to in this book. All links are for information purposes only and are not warranted for content, accuracy or any other implied or explicit purpose. No part of this may be copied, or changed in any format, or used in any way other than what is outlined within this course under any circumstances. Violators will be prosecuted.

Some of what is presented today may be too highly graphic for some people. Although our goal of this book is best summed up in one word – PREVENTION – our purpose is not to scare or frighten you. We have given special care to tone down the scary parts but the information presented is real and sometimes reality is not pleasant.

**Let's define terms...**

**Hackers** – a hacker is a criminal that usually wants to make a statement but generally does no major widespread damage and is not after financial gain. The group Anonymous is a good example. They are big at using "denial of service" attacks where they bombard a website's server until it crashes but it isn't about money.

**Crackers** – on the other hand, Crackers are evil and are strictly out for financial and evil gain. They are responsible for severe financial loss and stolen assets.

**Sexual Offenders:**

**Stalkers** – these are sexual predators bent on sexual crimes against men, women and children. Most stalkers only follow and record their victims while remaining hidden but some will cause bodily harm.

**Voyeurism** – These types of sexual offenders are better known as "peeping Toms" and get their thrills out of simply spying visually on their victims. They rarely take it further or cause bodily harm.

**Child Molesters** – these criminals prey only on children and haunt chat rooms, video game sites, and anywhere kids hang out online.

**Rapists** – these are very bad people and we can't put them away fast enough. They not only cause bodily harm, in many cases it is fatal.

**Exhibitionists** – these people get their thrills by exposing themselves to a certain class of people most likely women and children. They are essentially harmless and simply sick.

Important NOTE: Although males make up the bulk of sexual offenders, females make up some of the worst. Please bear this in mind.

YOU aren't the only ones being targeted! Every person, every corporate, religious and government entity is a target. Here are some examples…

If opening prison doors doesn't scare the pants off of you then think for a moment how many services you7 rely on that are controlled by computers. All of your water and food distribution is computer controlled. Your traffic lights, mail delivery, fire and police services and much more are all controlled by computers and all subject to hacking and cracking.

The Vatican as well as many organized religion sites is subject to hack attacks on a regular basis and most of these attacks originate in Muslim countries.

All financial institutions are targeted by hackers and crackers but financial institutions have some excellent cyber security protection in place so the most damage done is what is referred to as "Denial of Service" attacks where the goal is to hit a website with unlimited requests until it crashes.

Cell phone security risks take two basic forms – spyware intrusion where malicious spyware is implanted into the phone itself and also virus and malware infecting a phone from downloaded apps.

Whenever you surf the web, you open yourself up to a plethora of malicious spyware, malware and viruses hidden within the sites you are surfing. Most really good virus protection software can protect you like eSext.com but not all of them are virtually foolproof.

GPS tracking has many advantages but more disadvantages when it comes to spying and privacy issues. Later on in this book I will discuss this in detail.

The main thing to remember is that every time you log onto the Internet, you open your4self up to cyber crime UNLESS you take appropriate protective measures, which I will discuss later in this book.

Now, let's discuss how the government spies on you daily. A good amount of press has been devoted to this topic due to Edward Snowden's NSA spy revelations. Candidly, what was revealed about the NSA is nothing new; it is actually old news. And as I will point out, there are other government agencies that spy on you more than the NSA such as the DEA.

What is new is the extent of the amount of spying as well as the violations to the US Constitution, which makes much of the spying, conducted grossly illegal.

So let us begin at the beginning but get ready to be amazed…real amazed!!!

# Chapter 1 – Big Brother is Watching YOU

Government spying isn't accessing your computer and hacking your contents or implanting spyware on your phone.

They are directly wired into the Internet Service Providers (ISPs) and communication companies (cell phone service providers) and these companies literally turn over large databases filled with your info to the NSA and other alphabet spy agencies.

The trick in preventing this is called an "eraser' in forensics' lingo where all of your info, communications, pics and messages are wiped cleaned when you log off of any ISP, website, etc.

On your personal computer or cell phone, you have the ability to erase information but it is not completely erased and in most cases it can be recovered. In forensics, the erasers we use completely wipes everything clean and nothing can be recovered.

So there is a downside; we can do this for you under our FoneBlock and TechBlock programs (these products and programs can be found in the ForensicsNation Catalog listed in the back of this book) as long as you understand that nothing can be recovered!!!

Here is an article you will find most interesting from the Wall Street Journal:

**'Stingray' Phone Tracker Fuels Constitutional Clash**
http://online.wsj.com/article/SB10001424053111904194
604576583112723197574.html

For more than a year, federal authorities pursued a man they called simply "the Hacker." Only after using a little known cellphone-tracking device—a stingray—were they able to zero in on a California home and make the arrest.

Stingrays are designed to locate a mobile phone even when it's not being used to make a call. The Federal Bureau of Investigation considers the devices to be so critical that it has a policy of deleting the data gathered in their use, mainly to keep suspects in the dark about their capabilities, an FBI official told The Wall Street Journal in response to inquiries.

A stingray's role in nabbing the alleged "Hacker"— Daniel David Rigmaiden—is shaping up as a possible test of the legal standards for using these devices in investigations. The FBI says it obtains appropriate court approval to use the device.

Stingrays are one of several new technologies used by law enforcement to track people's locations, often without a search warrant. These techniques are driving a constitutional debate about whether the Fourth Amendment, which prohibits unreasonable searches and seizures, but which was written before the digital age, is keeping pace with the times.

On Nov. 8, the Supreme Court will hear arguments over whether or not police need a warrant before secretly installing a GPS device on a suspect's car and tracking him for an extended period. In both the Senate and House, new bills would require a warrant before tracking a cellphone's location.

And on Thursday in U.S. District Court of Arizona, Judge David G. Campbell is set to hear a request by Mr. Rigmaiden, who is facing fraud charges, to have information about the government's secret techniques

15

disclosed to him so he can use it in his defense. Mr. Rigmaiden maintains his innocence and says that using stingrays to locate devices in homes without a valid warrant "disregards the United States Constitution" and is illegal.

His argument has caught the judge's attention. In a February hearing, according to a transcript, Judge Campbell asked the prosecutor, "Were there warrants obtained in connection with the use of this device?"

The prosecutor, Frederick A. Battista, said the government obtained a "court order that satisfied [the] language" in the federal law on warrants. The judge then asked how an order or warrant could have been obtained without telling the judge what technology was being used. Mr. Battista said: "It was a standard practice, your honor."

Judge Campbell responded that it "can be litigated whether those orders were appropriate."

On Thursday the government will argue it should be able to withhold details about the tool used to locate Mr. Rigmaiden, according to documents filed by the prosecution. In a statement to the Journal, Sherry Sabol, Chief of the Science & Technology Office for the FBI's Office of General Counsel, says that information about stingrays and related technology is "considered Law Enforcement Sensitive, since its public release could harm law enforcement efforts by compromising future use of the equipment."

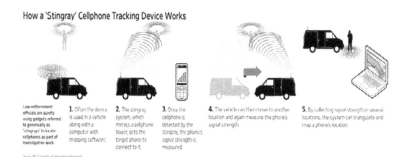

How a 'Stingray' Cellphone Tracking Device Works

**Law-enforcement officials are quietly using gadgets referred to generically as 'stingrays' to locate cellphones as part of investigative work.**

**1.** Often the device is used in a vehicle along with a computer with mapping software.

**2.** The stingray system, which mimics a cellphone tower, gets the target phone to connect to it.

**3.** Once the cellphone is detected by the stingray, the phone's signal strength is measured.

**4.** The vehicle can then move to another location and again measure the phone's signal strength.

**5.** By collecting signal strength at several locations, the system can triangulate and map a phone's location.

Source: WSJ research and government documents

The prosecutor, Mr. Battista, told the judge that the government worries that disclosure would make the gear "subject to being defeated or avoided or detected."

A stingray works by mimicking a cellphone tower, getting a phone to connect to it and measuring signals from the phone. It lets the stingray operator "ping," or send a signal to, a phone and locate it as long as it is powered on, according to documents reviewed by the Journal. The device has various uses, including helping police locate suspects and aiding search-and-rescue teams in finding people lost in remote areas or buried in rubble after an accident.

The government says "stingray" is a generic term. In Mr. Rigmaiden's case it remains unclear which device or devices were actually used.

The best known stingray maker is Florida-based defense contractor Harris Corp. A spokesman for Harris declined to comment.

Harris holds trademarks registered between 2002 and 2008 on several devices, including the StingRay,

StingRay II, AmberJack, KingFish, TriggerFish and LoggerHead. Similar devices are available from other manufacturers. According to a Harris document, its devices are sold only to law-enforcement and government agencies.

Some of the gadgets look surprisingly old-fashioned, with a smattering of switches and lights scattered across a panel roughly the size of a shoebox, according to photos of a Harris-made StingRay reviewed by the Journal. The devices can be carried by hand or mounted in cars, allowing investigators to move around quickly.

A rare public reference to this type of technology appeared this summer in the television crime drama "The Closer." In the episode, law-enforcement officers use a gadget they called a "catfish" to track cellphones without a court order.

The U.S. armed forces also use stingrays or similar devices, according to public contract notices. Local law enforcement in Minnesota, Arizona, Miami and Durham, N.C., also either possess the devices or have considered buying them, according to interviews and published requests for funding.

The sheriff's department in Maricopa County, Ariz., uses the equipment "about on a monthly basis," says Sgt. Jesse Spurgin. "This is for location only. We can't listen in on conversations," he says.

Sgt. Spurgin says officers often obtain court orders, but not necessarily search warrants, when using the device.

To obtain a search warrant from a court, officers as a rule need to show "probable cause," which is generally defined as a reasonable belief, based on factual evidence, that a crime was committed. Lesser standards apply to other court orders.

A spokeswoman with the Bureau of Criminal Apprehension in Minnesota says officers don't need to seek search warrants in that state to use a mobile tracking device because it "does not intercept communication, so no wiretap laws would apply."

FBI and Department of Justice officials have also said that investigators don't need search warrants. Associate Deputy Attorney General James A. Baker and FBI General Counsel Valerie E. Caproni both said at a panel at the Brookings Institution in May that devices like these fall into a category of tools called "pen registers," which require a lesser order than a warrant. Pen registers gather signals from phones, such as phone numbers dialed, but don't receive the content of the communications.

To get a pen-register order, investigators don't have to show probable cause. The Supreme Court has ruled that use of a pen register doesn't require a search warrant because it doesn't involve interception of conversations.

But with cellphones, data sent includes location information, making the situation more complicated because some judges have found that location information is more intrusive than details about phone numbers dialed. Some courts have required a slightly higher standard for location information, but not a warrant, while others have held that a search warrant is necessary.

The prosecution in the Rigmaiden case says in court documents that the "decisions are made on a case-by-case basis" by magistrate and district judges. Court records in other cases indicate that decisions are mixed, and cases are only now moving through appellate courts.

The FBI advises agents to work with federal prosecutors locally to meet the requirements of their particular district or judge, the FBI's Ms. Sabol says. She also says it is FBI policy to obtain a search warrant if the FBI believes the technology "may provide information on an individual while that person is in a location where he or she would have a reasonable expectation of privacy."

Experts say lawmakers and the courts haven't yet settled under what circumstances locating a person or device constitutes a search requiring a warrant. Tracking people when they are home is particularly sensitive because the Fourth Amendment specifies that people have a right to be secure against unreasonable searches in their "houses."

"The law is uncertain," says Orin Kerr, a professor at George Washington University Law School and former computer-crime attorney at the Department of Justice. Mr. Kerr, who has argued that warrants should be required for some, but not all, types of location data, says that the legality "should depend on the technology."

In the case of Mr. Rigmaiden, the government alleges that as early as 2005, he began filing fraudulent tax returns online. Overall, investigators say, Mr. Rigmaiden electronically filed more than 1,900 fraudulent tax returns as part of a $4 million plot.

Federal investigators say they pursued Mr. Rigmaiden "through a virtual labyrinth of twists and turns." Eventually, they say they linked Mr. Rigmaiden to use of a mobile-broadband card, a device that lets a computer connect to the Internet through a cellphone network.

Investigators obtained court orders to track the broadband card. Both orders remain sealed, but portions of them have been quoted by the defense and the prosecution.

These two documents are central to the clash in the Arizona courtroom. One authorizes a "pen register" and clearly isn't a search warrant. The other document is more complex. The prosecution says it is a type of search warrant and that a finding of probable cause was made.

But the defense argues that it can't be a proper search warrant, because among other things it allowed investigators to delete all the tracking data collected, rather than reporting back to the judge.

Legal experts who spoke with the Journal say it is difficult to evaluate the order, since it remains sealed. In general, for purposes of the Fourth Amendment, the finding of probable cause is most important in determining whether a search is reasonable because that requirement is specified in the Constitution itself, rather than in legal statutes, says Mr. Kerr.

But it is "odd" for a search warrant to allow deletion of evidence before a case goes to trial, says Paul Ohm, a professor at the University of Colorado Law School and a former computer-crime attorney at the Department of Justice. The law governing search warrants specifies how the warrants are to be executed and generally requires information to be returned to the judge.

Even if the court finds the government's actions acceptable under the Fourth Amendment, deleting the data is "still something we might not want the FBI doing," Mr. Ohm says.

The government says the data from the use of the stingray has been deleted and isn't available to the defendant. In a statement, the FBI told the Journal that "our policy since the 1990s has been to purge or 'expunge' all information obtained during a location operation" when using stingray-type gear.

As a general matter, Ms. Sabol says, court orders related to stingray technology "will include a directive to expunge information at the end of the location operation."

Ms. Sabol says the FBI follows this policy because its intent isn't to use the data as evidence in court, but rather to simply find the "general location of their subject" in order to start collecting other information that can be used to justify a physical search of the premises.

In the Rigmaiden example, investigators used the stingray to narrow down the location of the broadband card. Then they went to the apartment complex's office and learned that one resident had used a false ID and a fake tax return on the renter's application, according to court documents.

Based on that evidence, they obtained a search warrant for the apartment. They found the broadband card connected to a computer.

Mr. Rigmaiden, who doesn't confirm or deny ownership of the broadband card, is arguing he should be given information about the device and about other aspects of the mission that located him.

In the February hearing, Judge Campbell said he might need to weigh the government's claim of privilege against the defendant's Fourth Amendment rights, and asked the prosecution, "How can we litigate in this case whether this technology that was used in this case violates the Fourth Amendment without knowing precisely what it can do?"

**Write to** Jennifer Valentino-DeVries at Jennifer.Valentino-DeVries@wsj.com

\*\*\*\*\*

## Private Snoops Find GPS Trail Legal to Follow

http://www.nytimes.com/2012/01/29/us/gps-devices-are-being-used-to-track-cars-and-errant-spouses.html?pagewanted=2&_r=1&nl=todaysheadlines&emc=tha23

By ERIK ECKHOLM

Only yesterday it was the exotic stuff of spy shows: flip on a computer and track the enemy's speeding car.

Yasir Afifi of San Jose, Calif., showing where he found a GPS device the police had put on his car.

Online, and soon in big-box stores, you can buy a device no bigger than a cigarette pack, attach it to a car without the driver's knowledge and watch the vehicle's travels — and stops — at home on your laptop.

But today, anyone with $300 can compete with Jack Bauer. Online, and soon in big-box stores, you can buy a device no bigger than a cigarette pack, attach it to a car without the driver's knowledge and watch the vehicle's travels — and stops — at home on your laptop.

Tens of thousands of Americans are already doing just that, with little oversight, for purposes as seemingly benign as tracking an elderly parent with dementia or a risky teenage driver, or as legally and ethically charged as spying on a spouse or an employee — or for outright criminal stalking.

The advent of Global Positioning System tracking devices has been a boon to law enforcement, making it easier and safer, for example, for agents to link drug dealers to kingpins.

Last Monday, in a decision seen as a first step toward setting boundaries for law enforcement, the Supreme Court held that under the Fourth Amendment of the Constitution, placing a GPS tracker on a vehicle is a search. Police departments around the country say they will be more likely to seek judicial approval before using the devices, if they were not already doing so.

Still, sales of GPS trackers to employers and individuals, for a multitude of largely unregulated uses, are growing fast, raising new questions about privacy and a legal system that has not kept pace with technology. This easy tool for recording a person's every move is a powerful one that, when misused, amounts to "electronic stalking," in the words of one private investigator.

"That, to the victim, is just as terrifying as seeing your face in the window at night before they go to bed," said the investigator, John J. Nazarian, who heads an investigation agency based in Los Angeles.

So many suspicious spouses are now doing their own spying, a private investigator in New Jersey said, that his infidelity business is declining.

In the absence of legislation in most states, putting a GPS device on a spouse's car, or hiring an investigator to do so, is widely considered to be legal if the person placing it shares ownership of the car. But some privacy experts question this standard, and there is little to stop a jealous suitor, or an abusive man trying to prevent a battered woman from escaping, from doing the same.

GPS trackers are increasingly being cited in cases of criminal stalking and civil violations of privacy.

One increasing use of GPS tracking — by as many as 30,000 parents, one seller estimates — is to monitor the driving habits of teenagers; some devices even send a text message when the car goes over a certain speed.

Jimmie Mesis, a private investigator in New Jersey who, with his wife, Rosemarie, publishes PI Magazine and also sells devices through a company called PIgear, recalled a couple whose 17-year-old daughter had a drug problem and would disappear for hours at a time. Worried that she might overdose, they placed a tracker on her car. When they saw that she was visiting the same house repeatedly, they informed the police, who raided the drug den.

Also rising is the placement of devices in the cars or pockets of elderly parents with dementia. Mr. Mesis said one client with an erratic 86-year-old father discovered that he had driven to the southern end of the Garden State Parkway in New Jersey, and they were able to retrieve him.

Even if done legally and out of concern for family members, the covert use of GPS devices poses ethical questions. "To have this as a routine tool strikes me as pretty chilling," said Jonathan Zittrain, professor of law and computer science at Harvard University. "We are talking about partners and spouses, not pets."

"It cuts into someone's autonomy to know where they are all the time and not give them the opportunity to opt out," he said.

Rick Johnson, a private investigator in Denver, recalled two recent cases in which women who were going through divorces hired him because they believed that their husbands were following them. He found GPS trackers on their cars and removed them.

"It scared the hell out of these women," Mr. Johnson said.

Sales of GPS trackers to private individuals may have already surpassed more than 100,000 per year, some experts believe. The marketing is just getting started.

Danny Burnham, the general manager of InTouch MVC in Lakeland, Fla., said that he was negotiating with Best Buy, Radio Shack and Brookstone and that he hoped to be selling trackers in the big retailers before the end of the year. The devices will be described as safety tools, but no one can be sure of buyers' intentions.

"Selling a tracking device is similar to selling a firearm: you don't ask what they are going to use it for, and what they do with it is entirely out of our control," said Brad Borst, the owner of Rocky Mountain Tracking in Fort Collins, Colo. His company sells GPS devices online, including a 4-inch-by-2.5-inch model called the Ghost Rider, for $349 that can, with a waterproof box and magnet ($30), be hidden under a vehicle.

One Los Angeles man who went through a nasty divorce said he used zip ties to attach a similar device to the car his wife was driving, which was registered in his name.

He suspected that his wife, who had said she had health issues and could not work, was giving false testimony.

"I couldn't eat, I couldn't sleep, and then I got that thing," the man said. "It showed the car at the place of business. It showed that she was going out to nice restaurants. It showed she was living a lifestyle above what she had when she split up with me."

The man confronted his wife but never told her how he learned of her lies. In the divorce case, he said, "it was a major tool in saving my assets."

The most pervasive use of the devices is by companies that track fleets of vehicles or high-value shipments. But company detectives have also been making covert use of GPS devices to follow employees suspected of theft or malingering.

Paul J. Ciolino, whose Chicago-based investigation firm specializes in corporate work, recalled following an employee of one company who turned out to be playing golf every day. "He'd sit in the clubhouse and fill out expense reports for places he never went."

Some devices plug in under the dashboard and are powered by the car battery; others have batteries for covert placement. They establish position through satellite signals, and then report via cellphone towers to a central computer; customers, who pay perhaps $20 a month, log in to the server.

"To follow someone in a city like Los Angeles, law enforcement use 10 to 12 cars and even a helicopter, and even then they can still lose them," said Mr. Nazarian, the Los Angeles private investigator. "With this device, you apply it in 10 minutes, go have dinner, have a drink, then go see everywhere that car went, how long they stayed there. It's absolutely the cat's meow."

California and Texas, unlike most states, ban many uses of GPS trackers without consent, with exceptions for law enforcement and car owners. Many private investigators said they followed the same rules to minimize the risks of civil litigation — that a tracked person could sue for violation of privacy.

Niall Cronnolly, the president of Eagle Investigative Services, based in Atlanta, said his company uses GPS trackers in about half of the 3,000 to 5,000 cases it handles each year. Most involve suspicious spouses, he said, but sometimes employers track suspect workers. Mr. Cronnolly said the company uses the devices only when clients are married or engaged to the target or for employers only when the suspect is driving a company car.

"So in a sense," he said, "it's like putting a GPS device on your own car."

*Reporting was contributed by Jess Bidgood from Boston, Robbie Brown from Atlanta, Dan Frosch from Denver, Ian Lovett from Los Angeles and Steven Yaccino from Chicago.*

## Chapter 2 – Some That Didn't Get Away

Confessions of a Child Predator

An interview with a convicted child predator who caused the death of 5-teenagers

http://www.amazon.com/dp/B007BB97KU

In August 2006 a woman, under the moniker of Johnny B Goode, began accessing teen chat rooms and posing as a young male teenager.

Over an 8-month period, she was responsible for 5 teen suicide deaths caused by cyber-bullying. Law Enforcement was unable to determine her identity or her location.

She operated through a series of offshore proxies based in China and then only through computers she hijacked, effectively hiding her identity and location.

On September 26, 2006, she and her mother accomplice were behind bars.

## The Honeymoon Bandit

In the first quarter of 2007, a man known as the "honeymoon bandit" began preying on women that he befriended in online dating sites.

He would marry them, steal all of their assets and then disappear and begin all over again.

It took 10-months to track him down and apprehend him but only after he had married 14-women and had stolen their assets.

## Check these out on Amazon.com

Online dating sites are filled with hackers and crackers along with sexual predators. ALWAYS CHECK OUT WHO YOU ARE DEALING WITH!!! We can do this for you and read the books below to discover the perils of cyber dating.

http://www.amazon.com/dp/B006J9T4NA

http://www.amazon.com/dp/B006J9EMH8

## Hackman1

In the summer of 2008, a hacker known as "Hackman1" began illegally accessing various corporate databases and stealing personal and financial data in order to commit identity theft. In the course of a 6-month investigation, he was responsible for over 5566 victims totaling over $15-million in damages. When he was apprehended, he was on a yacht off the Florida Keys committing more identity theft.

*****

The unfortunate fact of this chapter is that too many hackers do get away and there is no way around this problem with the exception of the concept of prevention.

It is just too easy and too lucrative to become a hacker and/or cracker. Here is an article that will blow you away...

**Opinion: Difficult to become a hacker? It's easier than you think**
**With Symantec's Web client for pcANYWHERE, you can hack away without really trying.**

http://www.cnn.com/TECH/computing/9902/12/hack.idg/

February 12, 1999
by Mark Gibbs

(IDG) -- Ever wonder how hard it is to become a hacker? I can tell you firsthand it's probably easier than you may think.

It all started when I was testing Symantec's Web clients for pcANYWHERE on my office network. I downloaded the software from Symantec's site and ran it. Wonder of wonders, it worked perfectly -- way cool and very impressive.

As I was about to leave for a conference I thought it would be useful if I could use pcANYWHERE to access my machines while I was away. So I decided to test it by dialing up an ISP and looping back to my office via my digital subscriber line connection.

Imagine my surprise when I ran the applet and was given a list of six pcANYWHERE clients of which only one was mine.

Aha! Let's see if anyone forgot to set a password on his or her copy. Lo and behold, there it was, 2 a.m. and one copy was unsecured. Suddenly I was observing the screen of someone else's machine! Wild.

The owner was in the process of using a speech recognition system to dictate a letter to his girlfriend (no, nothing very steamy), and there at the bottom of the screen was his name (we'll call him Ralph).

I think the reason I could see his name was that it was part of the training data loaded into the speech recognition system. I thought I should let him know he had a security problem, so I put the cursor in the window his spoken words were appearing in and typed "Yo, Ralph." Nothing. He did not notice. I tried changing windows to Notepad but the speech recognition system switched back to the first window.

So to get his attention, I switched to my word processor, typed a long message, copied it to my clipboard, copied my clipboard over to his clipboard, and pasted the message into his active window. This time he noticed. He immediately pulled the plug on his computer, and the connection vanished.

I felt bad. I'd freaked Ralph out, and there was no opportunity to explain. So how to find him? Well, I knew his IP address but that was not much use so I went searching. Luckily he had an unusual last name, which made life easier.

I went to several search engines, including InfoSeek and AltaVista, and I found lots of dud leads (dead links and near misses). But eventually I hit pay dirt. I found a Web site and discovered what Ralph looks like (he has a picture of himself eating lobster) and that he is a scriptwriter. Then I went to switchboard.com and found him there, too.

From Ralph's Web site I knew where he'd been on holiday and some other trivia of his life. From switchboard.com I had learned Ralph's street address, telephone number and e-mail address. It had taken me all of 15 minutes.

So trying to be a nice guy, I sent him e-mail explaining what had happened, that I hadn't done anything to his PC, and noting that he should password-protect his copy of pcANYWHERE.

Next day there was no reply, so I called him. We had a non-conversation.

I explained who I was ("Uh-huh," he said), I assured him that I wasn't a hacker, ("Uh-huh"), that I hadn't done anything to his PC ("Uh-huh"), and that he should secure his system ("Uh-huh"). I explained that a hacker could have had a field day ("Uh-huh") and, well, I hardly got a response. Ho-hum.

It was such a simple hole in his system and one that I could have exploited without him having a clue what was going on. On the other hand, he probably wouldn't have been of much interest to a real hacker. But what if Ralph had been your chief financial officer? That could lead to all sorts of infiltrations into your corporate network. Frightening!

I would never have guessed that being a hacker was so easy.

Now let's discuss the so-called LEWGAL hacking conducted against you…

## Chapter 3 – Data Mining Your Personal Info is Legal

It may come as an extreme shock to you but there are companies that data mine your personal information and legally sell it to anybody including hackers and crackers.

These companies are so pervasive and invasive and they have some of the worst cyber-security features in place that protection of your personal information is a joke.

There are TWO main offenders that mine your personal info and both have had a number of security breaches…

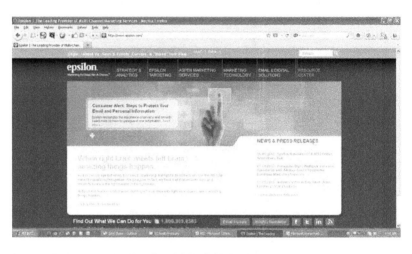

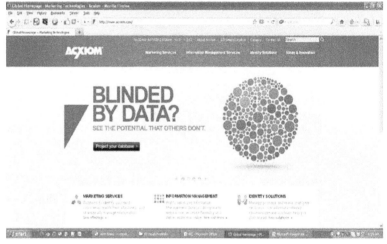

Here is a great article…

Nine Laws of Data Mining
By Tom Khabaza

http://khabaza.codimension.net/index_files/9laws.htm

*This content was created during the first quarter of 2010 to publish the "Nine Laws of Data Mining", which explain the reasons underlying the data mining process. If you prefer brevity, see my tweets: twitter.com/tomkhabaza. If you are a member of LinkedIn, see the "9 Laws of Data Mining" subgroup of the CRISP-DM group for a discussion forum.*

Data mining is the creation of new knowledge in natural or artificial form, by using business knowledge to discover and interpret patterns in data.

In its current form, data mining as a field of practise came into existence in the 1990s, aided by the emergence of data mining algorithms packaged within workbenches so as to be suitable for business analysts. Perhaps because of its origins in practice rather than in theory, relatively little attention has been paid to understanding the nature of the data mining process. The development of the CRISP-DM methodology in the late 1990s was a substantial step towards a standardised description of the process that had already been found successful and was (and is) followed by most practising data miners.

Although CRISP-DM describes how data mining is performed, it does not explain what data mining is or why the process has the properties that it does. In this paper I propose nine maxims or "laws" of data mining (most of which are well-known to practitioners), together with explanations where known. This provides the start of a theory to explain (and not merely describe) the data mining process.

It is not my purpose to criticise CRISP-DM; many of the concepts introduced by CRISP-DM are crucial to the understanding of data mining outlined here, and I also depend on CRISP-DM's common terminology. This is merely the next step in the process that started with CRISP-DM.

_____

_____

1st Law of Data Mining – "Business Goals Law":
   *Business objectives are the origin of every data mining solution*

This defines the field of data mining: data mining is concerned with solving business problems and achieving business goals. Data mining is not primarily a technology; it is a process, which has one or more business objectives at its heart. Without a business objective (whether or not this is articulated), there is no data mining.

Hence the maxim: "Data Mining is a Business Process".

_____

_____

2nd Law of Data Mining – "Business Knowledge Law":
*Business knowledge is central to every step of the data mining process*

This defines a crucial characteristic of the data mining process. A naive reading of CRISP-DM would see business knowledge used at the start of the process in defining goals, and at the end of the process in guiding deployment of results. This would be to miss a key property of the data mining process, that business knowledge has a central role in every step.

For convenience I use the CRISP-DM phases to illustrate:

· Business understanding must be based on business knowledge, and so must the mapping of business objectives to data mining goals. (This mapping is also based on data knowledge data mining knowledge).
· Data understanding uses business knowledge to understand which data is related to the business problem, and how it is related.
· Data preparation means using business knowledge to shape the data so that the required business questions can be asked and answered. (For further detail see the 3rd Law – the Data Preparation law).
· Modelling means using data mining algorithms to create predictive models and interpreting both the models and their behaviour in business terms – that is, understanding their business relevance.
· Evaluation means understanding the business impact of using the models.
· Deployment means putting the data mining results to work in a business process.

In summary, without business knowledge, not a single step of the data mining process can be effective; there are no "purely technical" steps. Business knowledge guides the process towards useful results, and enables the recognition of those results that are useful. Data mining is an iterative process, with business knowledge at its core, driving continual improvement of results.

The reason behind this can be explained in terms of the "chasm of representation" (an idea used by Alan Montgomery in data mining presentations of the 1990s). Montgomery pointed out that the business goals in data mining refer to the reality of the business, whereas investigation takes place at the level of data which is only a representation of that reality; there is a gap (or "chasm") between what is represented in the data and what takes place in the real world. In data mining, business knowledge is used to bridge this gap; whatever is found in the data has significance only when interpreted using business knowledge and anything missing from the data must be provided through business knowledge. Only business knowledge can bridge the gap, which is why it is central to every step of the data mining process.

---

3rd Law of Data Mining – "Data Preparation Law":
*Data preparation is more than half of every data mining process*

It is a well-known maxim of data mining that most of the effort in a data mining project is spent in data acquisition and preparation. Informal estimates vary from 50 to 80 percent. Naive explanations might be summarised as "data is difficult", and moves to automate various parts of data acquisition, data cleaning, data transformation and data preparation are often viewed as attempts to mitigate this "problem". While automation can be beneficial, there is a risk that proponents of this technology will believe that it can remove the large proportion of effort which goes into data preparation. This would be to misunderstand the reasons why data preparation is required in data mining.

The purpose of data preparation is to put the data into a form in which the data mining question can be asked, and to make it easier for the analytical techniques (such as data mining algorithms) to answer it. Every change to the data of any sort (including cleaning, large and small transformations, and augmentation) means a change to the problem space which the analysis must explore. The reason that data preparation is important, and forms such a large proportion of data mining effort, is that the data miner is deliberately manipulating the problem space to make it easier for their analytical techniques to find a solution.

There are two aspects to this "problem space shaping". The first is putting the data into a form in which it can be analysed at all – for example, most data mining algorithms require data in a single table, with one record per example. The data miner knows this as a general parameter of what the algorithm can do, and therefore puts the data into a suitable format. The second aspect is making the data more informative with respect to the business problem – for example, certain derived fields or aggregates may be relevant to the data mining question; the data miner knows this through business knowledge and data knowledge. By including these fields in the data, the data miner manipulates the search space to make it possible or easier for their preferred techniques to find a solution.

It is therefore essential that data preparation is informed in detail by business knowledge, data knowledge and data mining knowledge. These aspects of data preparation cannot be automated in any simple way.

This law also explains the otherwise paradoxical observation that even after all the data acquisition, cleaning and organisation that goes into creating a data warehouse, data preparation is still crucial to, and more than half of, the data mining process. Furthermore, even after a major data preparation stage, further data preparation is often required during the iterative process of building useful models, as shown in the CRISP-DM diagram.

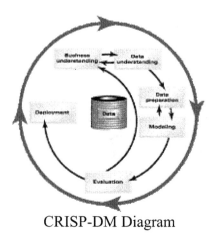

CRISP-DM Diagram

---

4th Law of Data Mining – "NFL-DM":
*The right model for a given application can only be discovered by experiment*
or *"There is No Free Lunch for the Data Miner"*

It is an axiom of machine learning that, if we knew enough about a problem space, we could choose or design an algorithm to find optimal solutions in that problem space with maximal efficiency. Arguments for the superiority of one algorithm over others in data mining rest on the idea that data mining problem spaces have one particular set of properties, or that these properties can be discovered by analysis and built into the algorithm. However, these views arise from the erroneous idea that, in data mining, the data miner formulates the problem and the algorithm finds the solution. In fact, the data miner both formulates the problem and finds the solution – the algorithm is merely a tool which the data miner uses to assist with certain steps in this process.

There are 5 factors which contribute to the necessity for experiment in finding data mining solutions:

1. If the problem space were well-understood, the data mining process would not be needed – data mining is the process of searching for as yet unknown connections.
2. For a given application, there is not only one problem space; different models may be used to solve different parts of the problem, and the way in which the problem is decomposed is itself often the result of data mining and not known before the process begins.
3. The data miner manipulates, or "shapes", the problem space by data preparation, so that the grounds for evaluating a model are constantly shifting.
4. There is no technical measure of value for a predictive model (see 8th law).
5. The business objective itself undergoes revision and development during the data mining process, so that the appropriate data mining goals may change completely.

This last point, the ongoing development of business objectives during data mining, is implied by CRISP-DM but is often missed. It is widely known that CRISP-DM is not a "waterfall" process in which each phase is completed before the next begins. In fact, any CRISP-DM phase can continue throughout the project, and this is as true for Business Understanding as it is for any other phase. The business objective is not simply given at the start, it evolves throughout the process. This may be why some data miners are willing to start projects without a clear business objective – they know that business objectives are also a result of the process, and not a static given.

Wolpert's "No Free Lunch" (NFL) theorem, as applied to machine learning, states that no one bias (as embodied in an algorithm) will be better than any other when averaged across all possible problems (datasets). This is because, if we consider all possible problems, their solutions are evenly distributed, so that an algorithm (or bias) which is advantageous for one subset will be disadvantageous for another. This is strikingly similar to what all data miners know, that no one algorithm is the right choice for every problem. Yet the problems or datasets tackled by data mining are anything but random and most unlikely to be evenly distributed across the space of all possible problems – they represent a very biased sample, so why should the conclusions of NFL apply? The answer relates to the factors given above: because problem spaces are initially unknown, because multiple problem spaces may relate to each data mining goal, because problem spaces may be manipulated by data preparation, because models cannot be evaluated by technical means, and because the business problem itself may evolve. For all these reasons, data mining problem spaces are developed by the data mining process and subject to constant change during the process, so that the conditions under which the algorithms operate mimic a random selection of datasets and Wopert's NFL theorem therefore applies. There is no free lunch for the data miner.

This describes the data mining process in general. However, there may well be cases where the ground is already "well-trodden" – the business goals are stable, the data and its pre-processing are stable, an acceptable algorithm or algorithms and their role(s) in the solution have been discovered and settled upon. In these situations, some of the properties of the generic data mining process are lessened. Such stability is temporary, because both the relation of the data to the business (see 2nd law) and our understanding of the problem (see 9th law) will change. However, as long this stability lasts, the data miner's lunch may be free, or at least relatively inexpensive.

5th Law of Data Mining – "Watkins' Law": *There are always patterns*

This law was first stated by David Watkins. We might expect that a proportion of data mining projects would fail because the patterns needed to solve the business problem are not present in the data, but this does not accord with the experience of practising data miners.

Previous explanations have suggested that this is because:

- There is always something interesting to be found in a business-relevant dataset, so that even if the expected patterns were not found, something else useful would be found (this does accord with data miners' experience), and
- A data mining project would not be undertaken unless business experts expected that patterns

would be present, and it should not be surprising that the experts are usually right.

However, Watkins formulated this in a simpler and more direct way: "There are always patterns.", and this accords more accurately with the experience of data miners than either of the previous explanations. Watkins later amended this to mean that in data mining projects about customer relationships, there are always patterns connecting customers' previous behaviour with their future behaviour, and that these patterns can be used profitably ("Watkins' CRM Law"). However, data miners' experience is that this is not limited to CRM problems – there are always patterns in any data mining problem ("Watkins' General Law").

The explanation of Watkins' General Law is as follows:

· The business objective of a data mining project defines the domain of interest, and this is reflected in the data mining goal.
· Data relevant to the business objective and consequent data mining goal is generated by processes within the domain.
· These processes are governed by rules, and the data that is generated by the processes reflects those rules.
· In these terms, the purpose of the data mining process is to reveal the domain rules by combining pattern-discovery technology (data mining algorithms) with the business knowledge required to interpret the results of the algorithms in terms of the domain.
· Data mining requires relevant data that is data generated by the domain processes in question, which inevitably

holds patterns from the rules which govern these processes.

To summarise this argument: there are always patterns because they are an inevitable by-product of the processes which produce the data. To find the patterns, start from the process or what you know of it – the business knowledge.

Discovery of these patterns also forms an iterative process with business knowledge; the patterns contribute to business knowledge, and business knowledge is the key component required to interpret the patterns. In this iterative process, data mining algorithms simply link business knowledge to patterns which cannot be observed with the naked eye.

If this explanation is correct, then Watkins' law is entirely general. There will always be patterns for every data mining problem in every domain unless there is no relevant data; this is guaranteed by the definition of relevance.

---

6th Law of Data Mining – "Insight Law":
  *Data mining amplifies perception in the business domain*

How does data mining produce insight? This law approaches the heart of data mining – why it must be a business process and not a technical one. Business

51

problems are solved by people, not by algorithms. The data miner and the business expert "see" the solution to a problem that is the patterns in the domain that allow the business objective to be achieved. Thus data mining is, or assists as part of, a perceptual process. Data mining algorithms reveal patterns that are not normally visible to human perception. The data mining process integrates these algorithms with the normal human perceptual process, which is active in nature. Within the data mining process, the human problem solver interprets the results of data mining algorithms and integrates them into their business understanding, and thence into a business process.

This is similar to the concept of an "intelligence amplifier". Early in the field of Artificial Intelligence, it was suggested that the first practical outcomes from AI would be not intelligent machines, but rather tools which acted as "intelligence amplifiers", assisting human users by boosting their mental capacities and therefore their effective intelligence. Data mining provides a kind of intelligence amplifier, helping business experts to solve business problems in a way which they could not achieve unaided.

In summary: Data mining algorithms provide a capability to detect patterns beyond normal human capabilities. The data mining process allows data miners and business experts to integrate this capability into their own problem solving and into business processes.

---

7th Law of Data Mining – "Prediction Law":
   *Prediction increases information locally by generalisation*

The term "prediction" has become the accepted description of what data mining models do – we talk about "predictive models" and "predictive analytics". This is because some of the most popular data mining models are often used to "predict the most likely outcome" (as well as indicating how likely the outcome may be). This is the typical use of classification and regression models in data mining solutions.

However, other kinds of data mining models, such as clustering and association models are also characterised as "predictive"; this is a much looser sense of the term. A clustering model might be described as "predicting" the group into which an individual falls, and an association model might be described as "predicting" one or more attributes on the basis of those that are known.

Similarly we might analyse the use of the term "predict" in different domains: a classification model might be said to predict customer behaviour – more properly we might say that it predicts which customers should be targeted in a certain way, even though not all the targeted individuals will behave in the "predicted" manner. A fraud detection model might be said to predict whether individual transactions should be treated as high-risk, even though not all those so treated are in fact cases of fraud.

These broad uses of the term "prediction" have led to the term "predictive analytics" as an umbrella term for data mining and the application of its results in business solutions. But we should remain aware that this is not the ordinary everyday meaning of "prediction" – we cannot expect to predict the behaviour of a specific individual, or the outcome of a specific fraud investigation.

What, then, is "prediction" in this sense? What do classification, regression, clustering and association algorithms and their resultant models have in common? The answer lies in "scoring", that is the application of a predictive model to a new example. The model produces a prediction, or score, which is a new piece of information about the example. The available information about the example in question has been increased, locally, on the basis of the patterns found by the algorithm and embodied in the model that is on the basis of generalisation or induction. It is important to remember that this new information is not "data", in the sense of a "given"; it is information only in the statistical sense.

---

---

8th Law of Data Mining – "Value Law":
    *The value of data mining results is not determined by the accuracy or stability of predictive models*

Accuracy and stability are useful measures of how well a predictive model makes its predictions. Accuracy means how often the predictions are correct (where they are truly predictions) and stability means how much (or rather how little) the predictions would change if the data used to create the model were a different sample from the same population. Given the central role of the concept of prediction in data mining, the accuracy and stability of a predictive model might be expected to determine its value, but this is not the case.

The value of a predictive model arises in two ways:
The model's predictions drive improved (more effective) action, and
The model delivers insight (new knowledge) which leads to improved strategy.

In the case of insight, accuracy is connected only loosely to the value of any new knowledge delivered. Some predictive capability may be necessary to convince us that the discovered patterns are real. However, a model which is incomprehensibly complex or totally opaque may be highly accurate in its predictions, yet deliver no useful insight, whereas a simpler and less accurate model may be much more useful for delivering insight.

The disconnect between accuracy and value in the case of improved action is less obvious, but still present, and can be highlighted by the question "Is the model predicting the right thing, and for the right reasons?" In other words, the value of a model derives as much from of its fit to the business problem as it does from its predictive accuracy. For example, a customer attrition model might make highly accurate predictions, yet make its predictions too late for the business to act on them effectively. Alternatively an accurate customer attrition model might drive effective action to retain customers, but only for the least profitable subset of customers. A high degree of accuracy does not enhance the value of these models when they have a poor fit to the business problem.

The same is true of model stability; although an interesting measure for predictive models, stability cannot be substituted for the ability of a model to provide business insight, or for its fit to the business problem. Neither can any other technical measure.

In summary, the value of a predictive model is not determined by any technical measure. Data miners should not focus on predictive accuracy, model stability, or any other technical metric for predictive models at the expense of business insight and business fit.

---

9th Law of Data Mining – "Law of Change": *All patterns are subject to change*

The patterns discovered by data mining do not last forever. This is well-known in many applications of data mining, but the universality of this property and the reasons for it are less widely appreciated.

In marketing and CRM applications of data mining, it is well-understood that patterns of customer behaviour are subject to change over time. Fashions change, markets and competition change, and the economy changes as a whole; for all these reasons, predictive models become out-of-date and should be refreshed regularly or when they cease to predict accurately.

The same is true in risk and fraud-related applications of data mining. Patterns of fraud change with a changing environment and because criminals change their behaviour in order to stay ahead of crime prevention efforts. Fraud detection applications must therefore be designed to detect new, unknown types of fraud, just as they must deal with old and familiar ones.

Some kinds of data mining might be thought to find patterns which will not change over time – for example in scientific applications of data mining, do we not discover unchanging universal laws? Perhaps surprisingly, the answer is that even these patterns should be expected to change.

The reason is that patterns are not simply regularities which exist in the world and are reflected in the data – these regularities may indeed be static in some domains. Rather, the patterns discovered by data mining are part of a perceptual process, an active process in which data mining mediates between the world as described by the data and the understanding of the observer or business expert. Because our understanding continually develops and grows, so we should expect the patterns also to change. Tomorrow's data may look superficially similar, but it will have been collected by different means, for (perhaps subtly) different purposes, and have different semantics; the analysis process, because it is driven by business knowledge, will change as that knowledge changes. For all these reasons, the patterns will be different.

To express this briefly, all patterns are subject to change because they reflect not only a changing world but also our changing understanding.
Postscript

The 9 Laws of Data Mining are simple truths about data mining. Most of the 9 laws are already well-known to data miners, although some are expressed in an unfamiliar way (for example, the 5th, 6th and 7th laws). Most of the new ideas associated with the 9 laws are in the explanations, which express an attempt to understand the reasons behind the well-known form of the data mining process.

Why should we care why the data mining process takes the form that it does? In addition to the simple appeal of knowledge and understanding, there is a practical reason to pursue these questions.

The data mining process came into being in the form that exists today because of technological developments – the widespread availability of machine learning algorithms, and the development of workbenches which integrated these algorithms with other techniques and make them accessible to users with a business-oriented outlook. Should we expect technological change to change the data mining process? Eventually it must, but if we understand the reasons for the form of the process, then we can distinguish between technology which might change it and technology which cannot.

Several technological developments have been hailed as revolutions in predictive analytics, for example the advent of automated data preparation and model re-building, and the integration of business rules with predictive models in deployment frameworks. The 9 laws of data mining suggest, and their explanations demonstrate, that these developments will not change the nature of the process. The 9 laws, and further development of these ideas, should be used to judge any future claims of revolutionising the data mining process, in addition to their educational value for data miners.

*I would like to thank Chris Thornton and David Watkins, who supplied the insights which inspired this work, and also to thank all those who have contributed to the LinkedIn "9 Laws of Data Mining" discussion group, which has provided invaluable food for thought.*

## Chapter 4 – Cyber Crime Examples

# The New York Times

**False Tax Returns**

**With Personal Data in Hand, Thieves File Early and Often**

MIAMI — Besieged by identity theft, Florida now faces a fast-spreading form of fraud so simple and lucrative that some violent criminals have traded their guns for laptops. And the target is the United States Treasury.

J. Russell George, the Treasury inspector general for tax administration, testified before Congress this month that the I.R.S. **detected 940,000 fake returns for 2010 in which identity thieves would have received $6.5 billion in refunds. But Mr. George said the agency missed an additional 1.5 million returns with possibly fraudulent refunds worth more than $5.2 billion.**

From 2008 to 2011, the number of returns filed by identity thieves and stopped by the I.R.S. increased significantly, officials said. Last year, it was at least 1.3 million, said Steven T. Miller, deputy commissioner for services and enforcement at the agency. This year, with only 30 percent of the filings reviewed so far, the number is already at 2.6 million. The bulk are related to identity theft, Mr. Miller said.

**Teen recounts horror of abduction into sex slavery**
**Many young victims of human traffickers treated as criminals themselves**

For someone who's only 18, Shauna Newell is remarkably composed as she describes being kidnapped, drugged, gang-raped and savagely beaten. It is only when she talks about seeing one of the men who sexually assaulted her — free and unafraid of being prosecuted — that she starts to break down.

"I went out to the beach a few weeks ago and I saw the dude who raped me, and he just looked at me," Newell told NBC News, her voice choking. "Like, hey ... you ruined my whole life. You have scarred me for the rest of my life and you're just sitting there going on with your life like nothing is wrong."

**Child Abduction**

**FHP -** *Mall* **& Shopping Safety**
*http://www.flhsmv.gov/fhp/misc/christmas/mst.htm*

More than 100000 *children* are *abducted* every year -- often in *malls* or department stores, according to the National Center for Missing and Exploited *Children* ...

**The day I was almost *abducted* & killed by a *child* predator - Kanuk ...**
http://open.salon.com/blog/kanuk/2010/06/22/the_day_i_was_almost_abducted_killed_by_a_child_predator

Jun 22, 2010 – The day I was almost *abducted* & killed by a *child* predator ... So I went on my way and walked to the *mall's* record store. Remember those?

**Is a fifth grader old enough to go to the *mall* by himself**
*http://wiki.answers.com/Q/Is_a_fifth_grader_old_enough_to_go_to_the_mall_by_himself*

And don't forget that even adult women have been *kidnapped from malls*, as well as other public places, so why would you think your *child* would be an exception...

SulphurDailyNews.com

**Dreamboard**

This week, the United States Attorney joined forces with the Attorney General and Department of Homeland Security to announce the largest United States prosecution of an international criminal network.

What's even worse about this particular case **...** **the** criminal organization was developed to sexually exploit children.

Dating back to December of 2009, the investigation targeted 72 defendants and more than 500 individuals around the world for their participation in an online organization called, "Dreamboard."

This private, members-only online bulletin board was created and operated to promote pedophilia and encourage the sexual abuse of very young children.

If you have young children, you may want to pay close attention to the particulars of this case. Let us warn you, however, it's not pleasant, but it's reality.

Truth Lives a Wretched Life...

# The Washington Post
The Feds concerned about hackers opening Prison doors

# The New York Times
In Attack on Vatican Web Site, a Glimpse of Hackers' Tactics

**YAHOO! NEWS**

Minnesota Wi-Fi hacker gets 18 years in prison for terrorizing neighbors

**theguardian**

Feds versus the hacker underground: army of informers turned by fear

**The Daily Dot**
*Today on the Web*

¡Viva Anonymous! The hacker gang is back in Mexico

"I strongly doubt the kidnapping took place," said Lelar the chief forensics investigator for ForensicsNation, wh hackers and groups like Anonuymous. "The cartel are r Anonymous."

**THE WALL STREET JOURNAL**

'Stingray' Phone Tracker Fuels Constitutional Clash

**abcNEWS**

## LulzSec 'Leader' Turns on Fellow Hacktivists:Feds

**And then you have what is being called "Not-So Legal Hacking of your personal info**

Sinister truth about Google spies: Street View cars stole information from British households but executives 'covered it up' for years.

Work of Street View cars to be examined over allegations Google used them to download personal details.

Emails, texts, photos and documents taken from Wi-Fi networks as cars photographed British roads.

Engineer who designed software said a privacy lawyer should be consulted.

**Mail** Online

**Even the government is spying on you…if you use certain words. And we knew this long before Edward Snowden's revelations…**

Revealed: Hundreds of words to avoid using online if you don't want the government spying on you (and they include 'pork', 'cloud' and 'Mexico').

Department of Homeland Security was forced to release a list of offending words following a freedom of information request. The agency insists it only looks for evidence of genuine threats to the U.S. and not for signs of general dissent…yeah, right!

The words are included in the department's 2011 'Analyst's Desktop Binder' used by workers at their National Operations Center which instructs workers to identify 'media reports that reflect adversely on DHS and response activities'.

## The commonality of all these cases...

The cases above are examples of cyber-crimes conducted over the Worldwide Web or Internet.
Not all cyber-crimes are for financial gain but in many cases bodily harm and even death occurs as a result.

As large as ForensicsNation is - almost 22,000 people in 22-countires - we don't even scratch the surface when it comes to cyber-crime.

Even working with counterpart companies in other countries such as Group-IB in Russia, where we share information and exchange databases, cyber-crime still runs rampant worldwide and is increasing.

http://group-ib.com/
**At ForensicsNation, we go after the real bad guys...**

ForensicsNation is organized into special units with expert investigators concentrating on various cyber crime activities. Here are just a few - financial, government, personal, and child molesters.

These special ops teams are highly trained and highly motivated. Using technology not available to the general public, we infiltrate and gather evidence and intelligence. This is the definition of the word "forensics" - the gathering and preservation of evidence. We then turn this evidence over to law enforcement for arrest and prosecution. But it isn't easy; cyber criminals are highly organized...

**Cyber Criminals Are Organized**

Hackers have their own news organization, their own news network. They even have their own education system and even their own movie.

What's next? Locusts? Boils?

# How To Become A Hacker
Eric Steven Raymond

**Table of Contents**

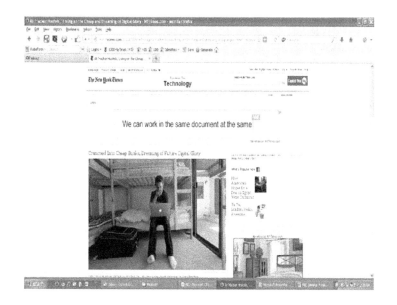

## Chapter 5 - Are Hackers Born or Are They Created Beings?

I want to demonstrate to you just how easy it is to become a hacker. Certain legislation has been proposed that makes it easy for hackers to be created. Here is an example of the government enabling hackers and crackers.

The **Cyber Intelligence Sharing and Protection Act** (**CISPA** H.R. 3523 (112th Congress), H.R. 624 (113th Congress)) is a proposed law in the United States which would allow for the sharing of Internet traffic information between the U.S. government and technology and manufacturing companies. The stated aim of the bill is to help the U.S government investigate cyber threats and ensure the security of networks against cyberattacks. The legislation was introduced on November 30, 2011 by Representative Michael Rogers (R-MI) and 111 co-sponsors. It was passed in the House of Representatives on April 26, 2012, but was not passed by the U.S. Senate

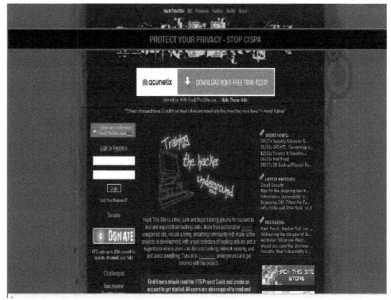

**CISPA means the "Cyber Intelligence Sharing and Protection Act"**

**"Hunting is for fools that have never heard about bait!"**

Actually the Hacker Underground is complete with their own news sites, news networks and these are really good things. These sites are where hackers BUY their information from other hackers. Info such as identity theft financial records, social security numbers, etc. So, we pose as buyers or sellers and "bait" the hackers. When they respond we plant a tracking bug into their computer systems and instantly they go into our databases.

Now you may ask how hackers pay for this information without revealing their identities. They use the following pay sites but even their systems are not that secure (lol). They also like using offshore pay sites because they are outside the regulations of The Patriot Act.

**The Problem?**

So far we have briefly described some of the potential crimes you are facing. The overall problem can best be outlined using two scenarios. First is hacking or spying on your information and personal data. Second is tracking your movements using GPS technology that can result in stalking and/or bodily harm.

Both can be stopped; both can be avoided and prevented. Now we are going to show you how to take control of your privacy and protect yourself, your business and loved ones.

This isn't difficult and it is not expensive but it is necessary! Please pay close attention; privacy is a serious matter and protecting yourself from bodily harm should always be of primary concern.

**The Solution?**

In one word – **PREVENTION!**

And this where each and every one of you comes in!!!

By conducting our PinpointProtect® Prevention Program seminars, we educate the public and business owners of the dangers of cyber-crime and the best defense is still a good offense!

By offering our PinpointProtect® Prevention Program workshops, we can teach prevention and tactics to combat even the best cyber-criminals.

Today cyber-criminals are conducting illegal hacking, child predation, identity theft, and denial of service attacks, financial fraud, online scams, phishing schemes, data theft, corporate espionage and much more...

**Are you the prey or the hunter?**

**Who will keep the keepers themselves?**

Within the ranks of ForensicsNation and companies like ours exist some of the best hackers in the world. Coupled with this fact is having access to technology that isn't available anywhere in the world. What this means is that our internal compliance and legal teams spend most of their time policing our investigators and they follow a policy of reverse democracy – they are guilty until proven innocent.

Everything our investigators do is scrutinized and policed. If there is any doubt or question we are immediately notified and asked to explain our actions.

Is this policing and scrutiny justified? Oh yes!

**Give us 30-minutes and we can turn your life into a living HELL**

In 30-minutes we can:
- Access your bank accounts and steal your money
- Tap your cell phone, listen to your phone calls, read your text messages.
- I can track your movements using GPS
- I can learn all about you – where you live, where you work, your habits, if you are single or married, your kid's names and ages, EVERYTHING!
- I can access your social media and change your profile and pics
- I can post false information about you that will never come off the net.
- I can find out your religious affiliation, voting records, and more.
- I will know your car, license info, and insurance data.

In short, give us 30-minutes and we will know everything about you and you cannot stop us because all of this info is on the Internet and you will never know who we are because we can hide where nobody will find us. Now you know why our compliance people watch us very carefully.

**Although truth lives a wretched life, it outlives a lie every time!**

Sooner or later truth always prevails and our job at ForensicsNation is to find the truth.

We have a saying, "An investigation doesn't end until someone is in handcuffs!" and we are well known for our tenacity.

But as we said before, as good as we are we need your help to combat the ever-increasing rate of cyber-crime. **Forewarned is forearmed!**

So now, allow us to describe cyber crime in terms of how it can affect you and introduce you to our programs that protect you. All of what I am about to describe is in the aforementioned download portal that we will give you at the end of this presentation.

**Enter ForensicsNation...**

Because of the nature of what we do, our forensic investigators are cloaked in anonymity for their personal protection as well as their families. The PinpointProtect® Prevention Program is important and so are the prevention products that we introduce to combat cyber-crime. We have spent the better part of 32-years in Cyber-Forensics and we have a good deal experience with cyber criminal activity.

What makes cyber-crime so ominous is the fact that cyber-criminals choose to hide behind their computer terminals and never actually witness the damage and harm that they do. They are not just immoral but cowards with absolutely no empathy for anybody including themselves.

But it goes much further than simply being immoral and cowardly. The mindset of cyber-criminals is not always something easy to figure out.

One of the sister-divisions to ForensicsNation is   our behavioral science unit called Applied Mind Sciences.

**http://AppliedMindSciences.com**
With over a dozen doctor/scientists on staff, we rely on AMS to assist us in profiling perpetrators of cyber-crimes and their apprehension.

So without further ado, let's get into the program and begin with personal protection...

What is the #1 target of all hackers and crackers? Can you guess?

## #1 Target of Hackers and Crackers

## LAW ENFORCEMENT

**ForensicsNation's website is subject to hacker attacks hourly...**

And I mean HOURLY!!! And candidly we LOVE IT too! Why? Because every hacker attack is monitored and defended by our compliance people and our internal security people and we plant spy software on the hacker's computer to reverse engineer their attack. Now we have another hacker in our databanks to go after.

But most law enforcement agencies do not have our technology and protection so they are penetrated daily. Law enforcement officers worldwide have their cell phones compromised. At ForensicsNation, our investigator's cell phones are scanned hourly for spyware.

It truly is a jungle out there.

**Everything cops have and use is unprotected**

## Anonymous's release of Met and FBI call puts hacker group back centre stage

Activist collective's leak of 18-minute discussion embarrasses authorities and raises questions over how security was breached

Josh Halliday and Charles Arthur
guardian.co.uk, Friday 3 February 2012 11.37 EST

Anonymous' release of a phone call between the Met police and the FBI has embarrassed the authorities. Photograph: Bruno Webber/Rex Features

The hacking collective Anonymous has struck deep into the heart of one of its sworn enemies — the police — with the release of the recording of a conference call between the Metropolitan police and the FBI. In it, they discuss ongoing investigations and court cases against alleged British hackers; and now, courtesy of Anonymous, the world can listen in too.

# #2 Targets of Hackers and Crackers is YOU!

# Hackers and Crackers go after YOU in this order of importance

1. **Children** – predators are most active in child abduction and abuse.
2. **Women** – everything from stalking to voyeurism to sex slavery.
3. **Businesses** – small business are more often targeted due to less protective measures.
4. **General Population** – in the form of various cyber crimes such as identity theft, computer intrusion, and phishing scams.
5. **Government Agencies** – patient records on file with state record keepers getting hacked.

**Areas of Personal EXPOSURE**

- Credit Card Fraud
- Identity Theft

- Financial Scams
- Child Predation
- Computer Hijacking
- Malware, Spyware
- Electronic Voyeurism
- Viruses
- Keystroke Logging
- Phishing
- User Account & Password Theft
- Cell Phone Spying
- Online Auction Fraud – Ebay, etc.
- And much more…

The above areas of personal exposure are the more prevalent forms of cyber crimes directed against individuals. It is by no means a complete list.

**YOU are the target!**

**Surfing the Web -** One way that hackers get hold of you is when you surf the web. They put up enticing websites and as soon as you bring one up on your screen they are secretly downloading spyware onto your computer.

**Cell Phone Spying -** One of the easiest ways to become a victim of cyber-crime is by hacking into your cell phone and installing spyware.

Today's Cell Phone spyware does not require that the hacker have possession of your phone. They simply text or call your cell phone number and whether it is answered or not, it takes all of about 30-seconds to marry your phone to the spyware.

Spyware of this type is readily available on the open market.

Did you know that with the help of a simple, inexpensive device, anyone with access to your phone could read your private text messages (SMS), even if you have deleted them previously?

This device can even recover contacts and previously dialed numbers. There is also a device that costs a whopping $20 that will tell you the cell phone number of any cell phone within 40-feet of the device.

And "no" we are NOT going to tell you where to buy one!!!

**The #1 Personal Intrusion is Cell Phone Spying**

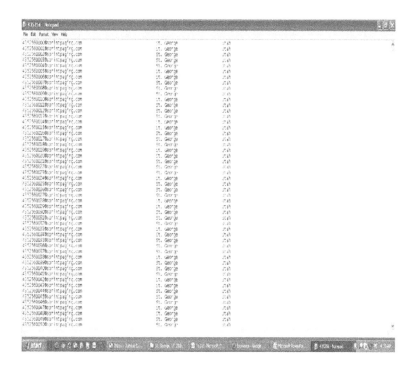

There are over 5.1 billion cell phone numbers in the world today and ForensicsNation has all of them in our database including yours. But the following slide is where most hackers go to find cell phone numbers...

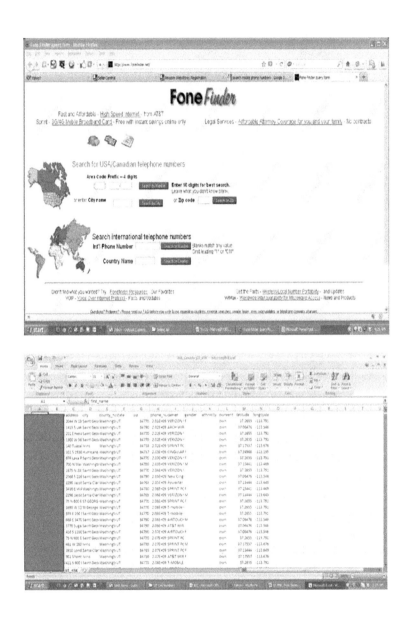

90

The above figure is a cell phone list is that you can buy on the open market complete with name, address and more. We have blocked out the personal names.

The above figure is an example of cell phone spyware available on the open market and it costs a whopping $15…sheesh! Once again we have blocked out the URL!

NO Waiting for the Mail
NO Shipping or Handling Charges
You will get immediate access to the
software once you have paid

Only $69.95 $15.00 FOR A LIMITED TIME!

DOWNLOAD RIGHT NOW!!

This is a DOWNLOAD PRODUCT

The website below tracks any cell phone in the UK 24/7. And no, we will not show you the US-based one so please don't ask!! There is a website for just about every country and believe it or not, these sites are FREE to use.

**Is it possible to buy services that are untraceable?**

The short answer is YES and NO!  I am going to introduce you to a cell phone service that is quite different from all of the mainstream services and then I will introduce you to another highly unique service most Americans know nothing about.

Later on in this book, I will introduce other services to you that are completely free that will assist you in staying "invisible" on the internet.

I strongly recommend that you consider using what I teach you today in order to prevent cyber criminals from accessing your stuff.

Straight Talk is available at Walmart and not only is it a great deal, you can prepay in advance quarterly, semi-annually or annually. Because this is a division of TracPhone, the information contained in the phone is generally not stored and since you do not need to give your personal information, it is safer than traditional cell phone services.

Private vaults do not take you personal information and do not even want to know your name. You gain access to your vault using retinal scanning technology. It is virtually impossible to seize the assets in your private vault because your name is not associated with the vault and you cannot sue an eyeball (lol). Sneaky, eh?

**You Know the Federal Government Can Legally Seize Your Stuff?**

You need to read this book.
http://www.amazon.com/dp/B007J4KH4O

It is a real eye opener and describes the legal mechanism the Federal Government can use to seize any of your assets especially food stocks. Do not fool yourselves!!! The government has seized assets in the past during the Great Depression. Precious metals such as gold and silver will be the first targets. Buy coins instead of bullion. Coins have been exempt in the past and never buy precious metal certificates; always take physical delivery of what you purchase.

**Cyber Criminals are waiting for you!**

**Email -** Your email accounts can quite easily be hacked. There is software available on the open market that breaks usernames and passwords. Also, if your computer is hacked, most people leave sensitive information on their computer that can fall into a hacker's hands.

**Hard Drive Intrusion -** Hacking your hard drive and other data storage devices can be prevented by using disc encryption programs.

**Other Areas of Vulnerability-** Firewalls, Internet Phone, Chat rooms, PORN, computer hijacking and much more...

DO NOT USE ANY OF THE FREE EMAIL SERVICES
SUCH AS GMAIL, YAHOO OR HOTMAIL!!! What
you want is a private email service like the one above that
you can access from the Internet under an "https" link.
ForensicsNation offers a secure and protected email
address with unlimited web access for just $4.97/month.
Example: suzie@forensicsnation.com.

To order, download the FNC Catalog here:
http://www.filefactory.com/f/d3eac5e74de46025

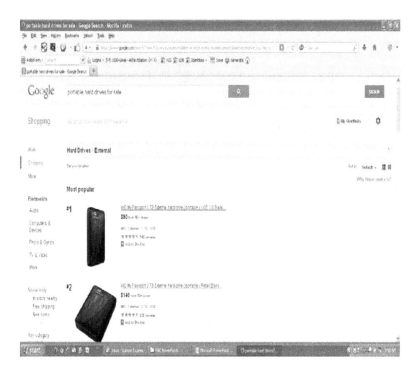

Instead of keeping all of your computer contents on your laptop or desktop's internal hard drive, use a portable hard drive like the examples above and just unplug it when you are finished.  By doing this, thieves do not have access to your stuff.  Never place ANY personal information on your computer's internal hard drive.

**Really Weird Stuff We Have Uncovered**

98

Electronic Voyeurism – Using a portable x-ray unit shown on the left, we caught a real "sicko" checking out women in a major department store.   This unit sees through clothing.   Where do people get access to this thing?  Ebay of course!

Wireless Camera – this little guy is only 1" X 1.5" in size and can be mounted anywhere like outside your window spying on you while you are getting dressed. It transmits to the Internet using cell phone antennas

This unit will tell the user your cell phone number and the user only has to be within 40-feet of your cell phone like sitting at a table next to you at Starbucks.

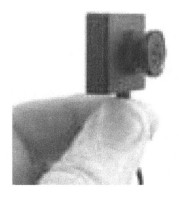

Button Camera – you only see the button and it records up to 12-hours. This unit also comes wireless and can transmit up to 300-yards. As small as it is; it can be installed just about anywhere. It even works in the dark!!! Furthermore, you can bet that within five years every law enforcement officer in America will be wearing one of these.

We caught one guy in his car with the monitor unit on the right using a button camera to spy on a "Hooters" waitress undressing in her apartment. Some people should get a hobby!

**CellPhone (Hands Free)
Voice Changer**

List Price: $20.00
On Sale Now: $19.00

For only $19, you too can call anyone and change your voice from male to female…too weird even for me!!!

**Email Interceptor
Software: Receive a cc
of all email**

List Price: $160.00
On Sale Now: $99.99
You Save: $50.01 (33 %)

Quantity: [ 1 ]

eBlaster is the ONLY software in the world that will capture their incoming and outgoing email and then IMMEDIATELY forward that email to you.

Who said your email was safe? This software can be installed remotely simply by sending you an email/text message.

This is a camera disguised as a Bluetooth ear piece used with cell phones. It also comes with a button camera and comes in wireless mode too!

We caught a woman in Starbucks listening in on a competitor's cell phone conversations and then stealing his business contacts. Simply plug it into your laptop and just listen in...whoa

**Two-Way Mirrors in Public Dressings Rooms**

Here is something to watch for that is more prevalent than you think – two-way mirrors in public dressing rooms. With shoplifting increasing at exponential rates, merchants are desperate to try ANYTHING to catch shoplifters EVEN if it violates your privacy.

Always check for two-way mirrors. Use a pen nib or your fingernail. Place it against the mirror. If the images touch it is a one-way mirror. If there is a gap between the images then it is a two-way mirror. The photo below shows a two-way mirror. Notice that the tips of the fingernail do not touch?

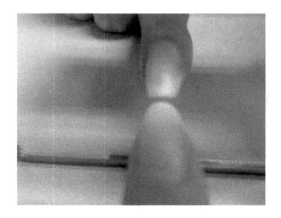

**The Ever-Increasing Cyber Problem**

The main problem is that the average computer user has no idea that they are exposed and even if they do, they have no idea how to protect themselves.

As technology expands, the tools available to the hacker and cyber-criminal expand too. They keep up with everything on the Internet where the average user does not.

Cyber-criminals are organizing into gangs. The most famous is the hacking gang called Anonymous that used "Denial of Service" techniques against major financial institutions that denied Wikileaks merchant account facilities in 2011.

But in countries such as Russia and many of the old "iron curtain" countries too, organized cyber-crime gangs are increasing.

## The 10-Most Notorious Cyber Gangs

1-Russian Business Network
2-Rock Phish Gang
3-NSA
4-Grey Pigeon Authors
5-Stormworm Gang
6-Awola Crew
7-DRG Group
8-South American Groups
9-Oga-Nigerian
10-Individual Hackers (Anonymous)

As cyber-crime increases, so does their income and this feeds the increase of more cyber-crime.

Like drugs, cyber-crime pays and it pays very well.

## Chapter 6 - Personal & Business Protection Solutions

Now we want to demonstrate some of the products and programs that ForensicsNation has created to protect you and your loved ones, business, etc…

**FNC Personal Protect**

The personal solution begins with consumer awareness and by understanding how cyber-criminals work. Not all cyber-criminal activities are conducted by organized gangs. A good many cyber-criminal activities are conducted by individuals.

ForensicsNation offers a product called **Personal Protect.** This is a comprehensive online PowerPoint presentation and webinar where you participate from the privacy of your home or office. It is taught by our Chief Forensics Investigator, who is considered one of the leading cyber-forensics experts in the world. He shows you how to protect you and your family when you surf the web, protect your email, prevent cell phone spying, hard drive encryption, the best firewall and antivirus programs to use, how to use secure chat rooms and much more. He provides you with all of the resources necessary to accomplish all of the above and most of these resources are FREE!

**PowerPoint Presentation Contents**
Antivirus Scans, Antivirus Programs
Backup Utilities
Disk Encryption
Email Privacy
Gamer Mode
Host-Based Intrusion Prevention System (HIPS)
Internet Browsers
Internet Security Training
Password Managers
Removable Media Control
Secure Hard Drive Wiping
Software Firewalls
Spyware Detection and Removal
Spyware Prevention
System Optimization and Privacy Cleaning Tools
Vulnerability Scanners
Vulnerability and Protection Techniques for Microsoft Office, PC Technician, Networking, Security, Web Design, Graphic Design, Data Management, Programming and Accounting

**Specific Areas of Protection**

There are areas that we address that affect your everyday computer usage. Legal and technology researchers estimate that it would take about a month for Internet users to read the privacy policies of all the websites they visit in a year. You know that dream where you suddenly realize you're stark naked? You're living it whenever you open your browser.

Your information can then be stored, analyzed, indexed and sold as a commodity to data brokers who in turn might sell it to advertisers, employers, health insurers or credit rating agencies.

And while it's possible to cloak your online activities fully, you can take steps to implement even the smallest of privacy and security measures.   Some of these measures are quite easy and many are free. Of course, the more effort and money you expend, the more concealed you are. The trick is to find the right balance between cost, convenience and privacy.  We show you how!

Before you can thwart the snoopers, you have to know who they are. There are hackers hanging around Wi-Fi hot spots, to be sure. But security experts and privacy advocates said more worrisome are **Internet service providers, search engine operators, e-mail suppliers and Website administrators** — particularly if a single entity acts in more than one capacity, like **Google, Yahoo, Facebook and AOL**. This means they can easily collect and cross-reference your data, that is, match your e-mails with your browsing history, as well as figure out your location and identify all the devices you use to connect to the Internet.

If you search on Google, maybe you don't want to use Gmail for your e-mail!

If you do not want the content of your e-mail messages examined or analyzed at all, you may want to consider lesser-known free services like **HushMail, RiseUp** and **Zoho**, which promote no-snooping policies. Or register your own domain with an associated e-mail address through services like **Hover** or **BlueHost**, which cost $55 to $85 a year. You get not only the company's assurance of privacy but also an address unlike anyone else's, like me@myowndomain.com.

Another shrouding tactic is to use the search engine **DuckDuckGo**, which distinguishes itself with a "We do not track or bubble you!" policy. Bubbling is the filtering of search results based on your search history. (Bubbling also means you are less likely to see opposing points of view or be exposed to something fresh and new.)

Shielding your I.P. address is possible by connecting to what is called a virtual private network, or V.P.N., such as those offered by **WiTopia**, **PrivateVPN** and **StrongVPN**. These services, whose prices range from $40 to $90 a year, route your data stream to what is called a proxy server, where it is stripped of your I.P. address before it is sent on to its destination. This obscures your identity not only from websites but also from your Internet Service Provider ISP). Moreover, these services encrypt data traveling to and from their servers so it looks like gibberish to anyone who might be monitoring wireless networks in places like coffee shops, airports and hotels.

Also, there is **Tor**, a free service with 36 million users that was originally developed to conceal military communications. Tor encrypts your data stream and bounces it through a series of proxy servers so no single entity knows the source of the data or whence it came. The only drawback is that with all that bouncing around, it is very S-L-O-W.

Free browser add-ons that increase privacy and yet will not interrupt your work flow include **Ghostery** and **Do Not Track Plus**, which prevent websites from relaying information about you and your visit to tracking companies. These add-ons also name the companies that were blocked from receiving your data (one social network, five advertising companies and six data brokers on a recent visit to CNN.com), which is instructive in itself.

Companies like Google are creating these enormous databases using your personal information. They may have the best of intentions now, but who knows what they will look like 20 years from now, and by then it will be too late to take it all back.

Download the ForensicsNation Catalog here with all our products and programs:
http://www.filefactory.com/f/d3eac5e74de46025

**FNC Corporate Protect**

## Taking the Fight to the Cyber-Criminals

From denial-of-service and web page defacements, to information theft that can cost your company millions of dollars, the motives and scope of attack may vary but the solution is the same. Understand the threat and implement appropriate countermeasures.

**FNC Corporate Protect** is a comprehensive online PowerPoint presentation and webinar designed to create security awareness and give business owners the unique skills required to protect the information assets of their organization. In this workshop you will learn what hackers know. You will learn what they can do, how they do it, and most importantly, how you can minimize or eliminate your vulnerabilities to these threats and attacks.

The premise of the **FNC Corporate Protect** is simple: you need to understand the threats to your business; you need to know what you can do to eliminate your vulnerabilities. As each exploit technique is taught, you will perform the task individually and then you will implement and test an appropriate countermeasure.

**Areas covered in FNC Corporate Protect include:**
1. Network footprinting, port scanning, and enumeration techniques
2. Specific operating system vulnerabilities
3. Web server vulnerabilities
4. Application level exploits, worms, viruses and Trojans Network vulnerabilities, sniffing, wireless sniffing, IP spoofing, and PPTP/VPN breaking

Two other critical areas presented in **FNC Corporate Protect** are **Intrusion Detection and Incident Response**.

As the names imply, these two areas address the tools techniques designed to give you the advantage of being prepared to deal with hacks if and when they occur. Being able to detect a hack and having a response plan in place will greatly improve your security awareness and further reduce your vulnerability. This course is delivered by ForensicsNation's senior security consultants, who bring real world experience to the classroom.

**Workshop Contents**

**Part 1: The hacker subculture and approach**
- An overview of the risks and threats
- An insight into the hacker underground
- The anatomy of a hack

**Part 2: TCP/IP fundamentals**
- TCP/IP and its relevance to hacking
- TCP header, flags and options
- UDP, ICMP and ARP
- Network traffic dump analysis
- Class exercises and lab sessions

**Part 3: Reconnaissance techniques**
- Selecting a target
- Identifying target hosts and services
- Network mapping techniques
- Fingerprinting and OS determination

- Scanning and stealth techniques
- Class exercises and lab sessions

**Part 4: Compromising networks**
- Vulnerability cross referencing
- Code auditing and insecure code examples
- Exploiting network services
- Sniffers, backdoors and root kits
- Trojans and session hijacking
- Denial of service attacks
- Trust exploitation and spoofing
- Buffer overflow techniques
- Web page graffiti attacks
- War dialers and dial-in hacking
- Manipulating audit trails and security logs
- Class exercises and lab sessions

**Part 5: Windows Applied Hacking**
- Windows components, Domains and structures
- Remote information gathering
- Scanning and banner checking
- Selecting services to attack
- Enumerating Windows information
- Windows hacking techniques
- Recent Windows vulnerabilities
- Class exercises and lab sessions

**Part 6: Windows effective countermeasures**
- User account policies and group allocations
- File and directory permissions
- File and print shares
- Hardening the registry
- Domains and trust relationships

- Securing network services
- Windows antivirus strategies
- Windows and Internet security
- Windows auditing and security logs
- Windows service packs and hot fixes
- Class exercises and lab sessions

**Part 7: Unix applied hacking**
- Unix components
- Unix variants
- Remote and local information gathering
- Scanning and fingerprinting
- Selecting services to attack
- Unix hacking techniques
- Recent Unix vulnerabilities
- Class exercises and lab sessions

**Part 8: Unix effective countermeasures**
- Unix password and group files
- User account and password controls
- Controlling command line access
- File and directory permissions
- SUID and SGID controls
- Crontab security
- Network and trust relationships
- Securing network services
- Unix antivirus strategies
- Unix and Internet security
- Unix auditing and security logs
- Unix security patches
- Class exercises and lab sessions

**Part 9: Network security strategies**

- Risk management and AS/NZS 4360
- Security management and AS/NZS 7799
- Developing a practical security strategy
- Physical security and environmental controls
- Personnel security and awareness training
- Firewall risks and strategies
- Intrusion detection system risks and strategies
- An overview of ecommerce security issues
- An overview of wireless security issues
- An overview of PBX security issues
- An overview of intrusion analysis techniques
- An overview of forensics procedures
- An overview of IT contingency planning
- Class exercises and lab sessions

**Part 10: Advanced Security Techniques**
- Inventory of Authorized and Unauthorized Devices
- Inventory of Authorized and Unauthorized Software
- Secure Configurations for Hardware and Software on Laptops, Workstations, and Servers
- Continuous Vulnerability Assessment and Remediation
- Malware Defenses
- Application Software Security
- Wireless Device Control
- Data Recovery Capability
- Security Skills Assessment and Appropriate Training to Fill Gaps
- Secure Configurations for Network Devices such as Firewalls, Routers, and Switches

- Limitation and Control of Network Ports, Protocols, and Services
- Controlled Use of Administrative Privileges
- Boundary Defense
- Maintenance, Monitoring, and Analysis of Security Audit Logs
- Controlled Access Based on the Need to Know
- Account Monitoring and Control
- Data Loss Prevention
- Incident Response Capability
- Secure Network Engineering
- Penetration Tests and Red Team Exercises

**Bonus:** Retina® Network Security Scanner from eEye.com. Recognized as the best scanner on the market in terms of speed, ease of use, non-intrusiveness and advanced scanning capabilities. Regularly priced at $1695, this is our gift for attending our webinar.

Download the ForensicsNation Catalog here with all our products and programs:
http://www.filefactory.com/f/d3eac5e74de46025

Pinpoint Protect

**PinpointProtect Child Watch**

**Children Are Exposed to Many Dangers**

Our children are our most valuable asset and yet very little is done to protect them from cyber-predators and criminal elements.

Not a day goes by that ForensicsNation is not working on a child predator investigation and the trending tells us it is getting worse.

Cyber-predators truly believe that they can remain invisible as they prey on kids and this is where they are very WRONG! ForensicsNation has caught some of the most notorious child predators.

Read "The Confessions of a Child Predator: http://www.amazon.com/dp/B007BB97KU

**Pinpoint Protect Child Watch** combines GPS technology along with the prevention techniques of ForensicsNation and acts as an electronic babysitter.

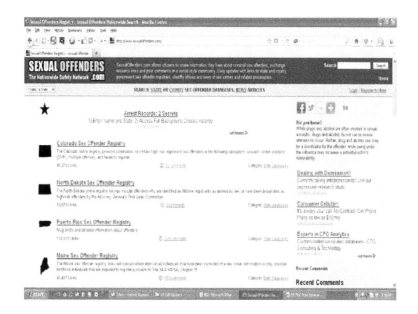

## Sex Offenders – St. George, UT

St. George, Utah is a small town in Southern Utah of 80,000 people and within a 2-mile radius of downtown St. George, there are 29 registered sex offenders. We don't worry about the registered sex offenders; the ones we are concerned about are the ones that FAIL to register.

**Pinpoint Protect Child Watch**

There are always situations that a person finds him/herself in that they cannot control.

PinpointProtect is here to assist you when you need help. If your child become lost, attacked, abducted, injured or has suffered through a disaster, we know where they are at all times and we can send help.

We know where they are because our proprietary GPS technology locates their exact position within 10-yards. We know if they are in trouble because all they have to do is push the "SOS" button and we go into action.

**24/7 Monitoring**

We monitor your child 24/7 through a state-of-the-art central control room where we scan the globe watching…ready to spring into action whenever we are needed.

It doesn't matter where your child is in the world; it doesn't matter how remote a location; the weather doesn't affect our ability to locate them; even if all services are down and unavailable, Pinpoint Protection is still working and still able to pinpoint your child's exact location.

**Password-Protected Internet Interface**
You may not know where your children are but we do! And everybody you give a username/password can pinpoint their exact location using our Password-Protected Internet Interface.

If your child is lost, you too can go on the Internet and find his/her location…and anyone else that you give permission to locate them. Again, it doesn't matter where they are in the world or the weather conditions; we always know where your child is and so does anybody else that you give permission to know.

**Here is how we do it…**

**The Problem:** the biggest problem concerning GPS tracking devices is the battery life. Most GPS tracking devices are only used for specific surveillance for a short period of time and hence; the battery life is only a few hours.

**The Solution:** Our proprietary tracking unit works on motion and will conserve battery power when a person is not moving. The unit has a battery life of 30 hours depending on the reporting rate you choose.

**This is important!** First, our unit goes to sleep as long as you are stationary. The minute you start moving, it wakes up and reports your coordinates.

This feature saves the battery life and allows our unit up to 3-days usage until it needs to be recharged (the unit comes with a charger and it works just like your cell phone charger).

Second, our PinpointProtect proprietary software in our control room automatically notifies our personnel when your child has been stationary for an unusually long period of time.

Our personnel check your child's location first to determine if there is a good reason that he/she have been stationary. For example, if your child resides in New York and he/she has been stationary after 8 PM Eastern Time, then we can easily assume he/she is sleeping.

However; if your family is camping in the remote desert of New Mexico and have been stationary for over 8-hours, our personnel will attempt to make contact with you.

If we cannot make contact then we will call the contact people on your application and inquire if they have been in communication with you. If we determine that no one has been in contact with you we send our people to find you.

**Furthermore** – there is no reason for the unit to be turned off. Even when it is charging the unit can remain on. Our PinpointProtect proprietary software in our control room automatically notifies our personnel when any unit is turned off and we immediately attempt to make contact.

Again, if we cannot make contact then we will call the contact people on your application and inquire if they have been in communication with you.

**Here are just a few of the devices we offer!**

**Note** – a customer can turn the unit off at any time if they do not want their location known. If the unit is attached to a child, this function can be disabled. This is your choice. If so, we provide a phone number to our control room to notify our personnel that you are turning off the unit so we do not react.

**Peace of mind** – Knowing that PinpointProtect personnel are just a phone call away is very comforting. For whatever reason, you can always call us for assistance and our personnel will respond.

Download the ForensicsNation Catalog here with all our products and programs:
http://www.filefactory.com/f/d3eac5e74de46025

**PinpointProtect Guardian**

**Affordable Protection for Everyone!**

If we lived in a perfect world, there would be no need for Pinpoint Protect Guardian. Unfortunately, just walking outside of your house is fraught with danger. Pinpoint Protect Guardian does many things but most of all it offers peace of mind and the ability to keep track of your loved ones 24/7.

So if your spouse travels on business, you know where he/she is all of the time. If you have elderly parents, Pinpoint Protect Guardian acts as an electronic babysitter. The uses and applications of **Pinpoint Protect Guardian** are endless. Here are just a few…

**High Profile People** – people with high profiles: movie stars, sports figures, wealthy people, government figures, etc. need extra protection and PinpointProtect gives them that special peace-of-mind.

**Lost** – everybody becomes lost eventually. It doesn't even have to be somewhere that is remote; if you are lost you can hit the SOS button or if you have access to the Internet, you can find your exact location.

**Attacked** – women are especially vulnerable to attack and eventually find themselves in situations where an attack is made easier such as parking garages, elevators, dark streets, parking lots. Just hit the SOS button and we send the cavalry.

**Abducted** – unfortunately, abduction and kidnapping has become a cottage industry in many parts of the world, especially in Mexico, Central and South America. If you live or travel to any parts of the world where this is common you need PinpointProtect!

**Injured** – In any situation where you are injured, even if you cannot push the SOS button, we at least know where you are and can send help.

**Disaster** – you can be buried under rubble and we still can locate you. You may not be able to communicate with the outside world because all communication facilities are down but your family can know where you are and if you are moving by logging into the Internet Interface. http://SurvivalNations.com

**Travel** – no matter where you go or where you travel to, PinpointProtect goes with you and gives your loved ones peace-of-mind knowing exactly where you are at all times. They can even know if you arrived at your destination by using the Internet Interface.

**Work** – do you have a job where you work alone or in a remote location? With PinpointProtect, you are NEVER alone! We are there with you at all times.

**Dating** – date rape and violence against women is becoming all too common. How does a woman protect herself? Yep…PinpointProtect! Now if a lady needs help she can push the SOS button and we send help to her exact location. But this doesn't mean that a lady should not be prudent and do all she can to protect herself.

**Banking** – If you take daily deposits to the bank for your business, you need PinpointProtect! Don't be foolish enough to think that no one is watching you and logging the times and routes you take to the bank. Plan for the worst but hope for the best!

**Elderly** – oddly enough, most of the "lost" calls we receive are for elderly people. With the advent of electric wheelchairs (scooters) the elderly have a tendency to wander. They are easily disoriented and need help. With PinpointProtect, it is easy to find them and bring them home. Also the SOS button is there in case they need help for whatever reason.

**Teens** – the best description for teens is "walking hormones with feet"! Let's face it; the world presents way too many opportunities for teens to get into trouble. One would think that teens resent PinpointProtect. Not so; our surveys show that they actually appreciate having the ability to communicate when they are in trouble and know that their parents know where they are at all times.

**College** – PinpointProtect gives parents that extra peace-of-mind when their kids go off to college. Knowing where they are and where they are supposed to be and also knowing that when they get into trouble or a scary situation that they have a way to communicate is comforting to parents whose kid(s) are out of the nest for the first time.

**Hunting** – all hunting takes place in remote locations and many times in locations where cell phones do not work. Never go hunting without PinpointProtect!

**Driving/Commuting** – no matter where you drive or how long a commute PinpointProtect goes along with you. Even if cell phone service isn't available, PinpointProtect is always available.

**Pets** – now you will never lose a pet. Just place the PinpointProtect unit on your pet's collar and you will always know where it is.

**The list is endless...**we simply cannot list all of the scenarios that PinpointProtect has been used. Our customers continue to amaze us on how they employ PinpointProtect!

**Dreamers covet the object of their temptation, BUT they covet <u>the temptation</u> more so than <u>the object</u> itself because <u>the temptation is the idol of their fantasy</u>.**

Allow me to teach you some behavioral science. All sexual predators are dreamers and the more they embrace a faulty fantasy life the more they spiral down into the pit of depravity. **This is important – what they covet is the temptation of the criminal act more than the object such as the woman herself or child.** This is why most sexual predators are harmless and cause no bodily harm. But some take their fantasies to the extreme and when temptation isn't enough they begin to act out their fantasies and this is when they become very dangerous.

**FNC Proprietary Products**

**FoneScan** – Using our advanced technology we can scan your phone remotely and then remove any malicious spyware. **Cost $19.97**

**FoneBlock** – Upon discovery of any malicious spyware, we can install our proprietary FoneBlock phone app that blocks any and all malicious spyware from being installed on your phone. Works on all handsets and remains hidden from any hackers. **Cost $29.97**

**TechScan** – We can remotely scan any desktop computer, laptop and/or tablet computer to discover any malicious spyware or adware. **Cost $29.97**

**TechBlock -** Upon discovery of any malicious spyware, we can install our proprietary TechBlock software that blocks any and all malicious spyware from being installed on your desktop, laptop or tablet. It works on any computer operating system and remains hidden from detection from any computer protection software such as Norton and MacAfee.
**Cost $49.97**

**Onsite HomeScan** – We will send a forensics investigator to your home and scan both the inside and outside of your home for cameras, bugs, etc. **Cost $99**

**Onsite BusinessScan -** We will send a forensics investigator to your business and conduct an internal audit of your computer systems and inside/outside premises. **Cost $499**

Download the ForensicsNation Catalog here with all our products and programs:
http://www.filefactory.com/f/d3eac5e74de46025

**Online Workshops**

**FNC Personal Protect** – every man, woman and teenager on the planet should go through this workshop. There is nothing like it taught anywhere. Learning how to protect yourself begins with learning what the dangers are that confront you and that you are not aware of that exist. **$197**

**FNC Corporate Protect** – protecting your business is protecting your source of income and prosperity. This workshop includes an online visit to your business from one of our Loss Prevention Officers to determine the areas you are most vulnerable. **Workshop + online consultation $497**

**Pinpoint Protect Child Watch** – protecting your children is a primary concern. This workshop alerts you to the dangers confronting children and is taken from actual case files of ForensicsNation. **$197**

**Pinpoint Protect Guardian** – learning how to protect your entire family – husband, wife, children, elderly parents and more is the topic of this workshop. Certain professions, travel, hunting, and much more are defined and solutions offered.
**$197**

**Pinpoint Protect Trained Observation -** you look but you do not see; you listen but you do not hear. The human mind filters out a good deal of incoming data. If you can't see or hear danger coming then you are what we call a VICTIM! This workshop teaches "trained observation" and how to correct the filters in your mind. After 4-hours of intense training you won't miss anything whether you see or hear it.
**$99 /person**

**Body Language & Body Talk -** One of the most needed talents in personal protection is deciphering what somebody is going to do and body language gives this away each and every time. Fight or flight is determined

by many things but body language gives you the advantage. This workshop is one of the most fascinating workshops we have ever created.
**$99/person**

**NOTE:** All of our workshops are taught online in ForensicsNation online classroom and each attendee participates from the privacy of his/her home or office. To see a list of available workshops and or to participate download the ForensicsNation Catalog here with all our products and programs:

http://www.filefactory.com/f/d3eac5e74de46025

**ForensicsNation Store Catalog**

We have taken the guess work out of identifying good quality products and the best prices by publishing our own catalog for your convenience.

All of the products contained in our catalog are used by ForensicsNation every day.

Download your FREE catalog and begin protecting yourself and your loved ones Today.
Go here for your FREE download:

http://www.filefactory.com/f/d3eac5e74de46025

ForensicsNation Catalog

Cyber Crime Prevention Programs and Products

ForensicsNation

141

### I Have a Special Gift for My Readers

I appreciate my readers for without them I am just another author attempting to make a difference. If my book has made a favorable impression please leave me an honest review. Thank you in advance for you participation.

My readers and I have in common a passion for the written word as well as the desire to learn and grow from books.

My special offer to you is a massive ebook library that I have compiled over the years. It contains hundreds of fiction and non-fiction ebooks in Adobe Acrobat PDF format as well as the Greek classics and old literary classics too.

In fact, this library is so massive to completely download the entire library will require over 5 GBs open on your desktop.

Use the link below and scan all of the ebooks in the library. You can select the ebooks you want individually or download the entire library.

The link below does not expire after a given time period so you are free to return for more books rather than clog your desktop. And feel free to give the link to your friends who enjoy reading too.

I thank you for reading my book and hope if you are pleased that you will leave me an honest review so that I can improve my work and or write books that appeal to your interests.

Okay, here is the link…

http://tinyurl.com/special-readers-promo

PS: If you wish to reach me personally for any reason you may simply write to mailto:support@epubwealth.com.

I answer all of my emails so rest assured I will respond.

**Meet the Author**

Dr. Treat Preston is a behavioral scientist specializing in all types of relationships and associated problems, psychological triggers as applied to commercial advertising and marketing, and energy psychology.

He is also one of the lead research scientists with AppliedMindSciences.com, the mind research unit of Forensicsnation.com.

He and his wife Cynthia reside in Auburn, California.

http://www.amazon.com/author/treatpreston

http://www.AddMeInNow.com
http://appliedmindsciences.com/
http://appliedwebinfo.com/
http://BoolbuilderPLUS.com
http://embarrassingproblemsfix.com/
http://www.epubwealth.com/
http://forensicsnation.com/
http://www.freebiesnation.com/
http://www.HealthFitnessWellnessNation.com
http://neternatives.com/
http://privacynations.com/
http://survivalnations.com/
http://thebentonkitchen.com
http://theolegions.org
http://www.VideoBookbuilder.com


**Some Other Books You May Enjoy From ePubWealth.com**

**FNC Bushwhacker Program $2.99**
**Kindle Version**
http://www.amazon.com/dp/B007I9AHVS
**PDF Version**
https://www.paypal.com/cgi-bin/webscr?cmd=_s-xclick&hosted_button_id=KMKHDMBQSZ4E4

Have you ever been hacked? Have you been a victim of Identity Theft? Has your computer ever been infected with a virus, malware, or spyware? Do you know who is reading your personal information, spying on your cell phone conversations and text messages?

The Internet is a fantastic tool that we all have come to rely on for a vast variety of needs but the Internet is a cesspool of cyber-crime and hackers bent on evil intent. From child predators that prey on kids in chat rooms to corporate espionage where corporate secrets are pilfered and sold for sizeable profits, cyber-crime is real and the cyber-criminals are very good at what they do.

How good are you at preventing them from practicing their evil trade?

The FNC Bushwhacker Program teaches you how to become the hunter instead of the prey. It also teaches you how to block cyber-criminals from accessing your personal information, protect your children, and catch the bad guys when they attempt to make you a victim.

Everyone should become a student of the FNC Bushwhacker program. It is that important!

FNC Bushwhacker Program comes in two parts. The second part is called the FNC Bushwhacker PLUS Program is an in depth course that makes you literally bulletproof to cyber-crime of all types. It provides all of the resources you need to become an "amateur internet sleuth" and this is a must instructional experience.

You cannot afford not to be without this information!

**You Can Run But You Cannot Hide $4.87**
**Kindle Version**
http://www.amazon.com/dp/B006JLVZC6
**PDF Version**
https://www.paypal.com/cgi-bin/webscr?cmd=_s-xclick&hosted_button_id=277UDEF7GYMK6

Protect Yourself Online – You Can Run But You Cannot Hide is all about cyber security online and computer security online. The book is packed with resources demonstrating computer security programs most of which are free to the user. The Internet is filled with hackers, scammers, fraudsters and criminal elements waiting to prey on you and steal your privacy, your money, your security, and in some cases even your life! You Can Run But You Cannot Hide tells you how they do it; how they patiently wait for you to become vulnerable and then they pounce. This book shows you the resources they use, their techniques and then shows you how to protect yourself and even how to become an Internet amateur sleuth. Now the hunters will become the prey. Protecting yourself from identity theft and demonstrating various identity protection services as well as credit fraud protection are two of the most common cyber crimes. Protect yourself today!

**Dropping Off The Grid $6.87**
**Kindle Version**
http://www.amazon.com/dp/B006JLGKLC
**PDF Version**
https://www.paypal.com/cgi-bin/webscr?cmd=_s-xclick&hosted_button_id=X6N67JYHPLWB6

Privacy Issues – Dropping Off The Grid is all about protecting your privacy and your loved ones from such things as identity theft, data theft, and consumer fraud. The identity thief is patient and lurks in the background waiting for you to slip up. ID theft prevention is easy and this book will give you resources on how to protect yourself and loved ones from all types of internet privacy issues. It provides valuable resources to protecting your privacy in a variety of situations such as Internet, credit, business and personal.

It is the only compendium of its kind that gives you everything you need to protect your privacy and all at your fingertips. Keep the criminal elements and stalkers at bay. Protect your identity, your finances and your privacy now. This Parenting and Family book is a one that the whole family can enjoy. Teach your children while they are young to guard their privacy. Make it a family activity. Privacy is a right! Know your consumer rights today!

**Child Watch $2.99**
**Kindle Version**
http://www.amazon.com/dp/B0095K1P3M
**PDF Version**

https://www.paypal.com/cgi-bin/webscr?cmd=_s-xclick&hosted_button_id=FLJM7KUKXKG6U

School Safety & Violence – Child Watch is all about protecting children from sexual predators and the many dangers they face daily. It provides true insight into cyber crimes and child predators. It was written by Chief Forensics Investigator and behavioral scientist, Dr. Leland Benton. He has spent the better part of 31-years tracking down and apprehending some of the worst child predators. No one is more qualified to tell this amazing story. If you have children then you need to read this book. If you have a desire to learn how to better protect your family and loved ones, Child Watch offers insight into the safeguards necessary to identify and block cyber criminals including sexual predators. It also identifies bullying in schools and offers bullying in schools resources and ways to stop bullying. It provides domestic violence education and ways to protect children from people they know that may harm them. Youth violence is at an all time high and Dr. Benton offers ways to prevent youth violence. He demonstrates school intervention programs and security for schools. Educate yourself in what exactly your children are facing and take steps to protect them now.

**Confessions of a Child Predator $6.87**
**Kindle Version**
http://www.amazon.com/dp/B007BB97KU
**PDF Version**
https://www.paypal.com/cgi-bin/webscr?cmd=_s-xclick&hosted_button_id=KJDUPJC8ZRR26

"Confessions of a Child Predator" is a hard core look inside the minds of two female child predators. As convicted sex offenders and murderers, they were serving life sentences without parole. The interview was conducted in prison by behavior scientist Dr. Harry Jay. Parents, you need to read this book because it contains information that will amaze you. Information like how your children are exposed daily to child molesters…DAILY… and how to protect them are all in this book. It is also imperative that you use various online sex offender registry websites and conduct a sex offenders search in your local area to find registered sex offenders that live close to you. More importantly, learn the child predator warning signs and keep a constant eye on your children and their environment.

**Cyber-Daters Beware $2.99**
**Kindle Version**
http://www.amazon.com/dp/B006J9T4NA
**PDF Version**
https://www.paypal.com/cgi-bin/webscr?cmd=_s-xclick&hosted_button_id=M8S965D4889X8

Cyber Dating Dangers – Cyber Daters BEWARE outlines the inherent dangers of online relationships beginning at various single sites and all of the stories are taken from actual case studies. Online singles – be afraid…be real afraid! Cyber dating isn't all as safe as they want you to believe. Both men and women need to protect themselves and their online personals information. How is online dating dangerous?

Cyber-Daters BEWARE shows you the inherent dangers and how to protect yourself from the predators that lurk in the background. Online dating scams abound on these single sites. Look for the clues! This book will teach you how to identify the clues. This Advice and How To book outlines the ways to protect yourself and what to look for if you choose to cyber date. It is all about safe online dating. Parents and families should read this book together as children become of dating age.

**Cyber Protect Your Business $4.87**
**Kindle Version**
http://www.amazon.com/dp/B0095JEAYY
**PDF Version**
https://www.paypal.com/cgi-bin/webscr?cmd=_s-xclick&hosted_button_id=596BMEK4NM6GS

Cyber Protection – Cyber Protect Your Business is about protecting one of your most important assets – your business and your livelihood. Statistics demonstrate that hackers are now targeting small businesses more so than individuals because the payoffs are greater and there are fewer safeguards put in place by the business owner. It is easy pickings and the business owners that take the time to read this book and implement the strategies contained herein will be the targets that the hackers ignore since there are easier targets available.
Cyber Protect Your Business is about protecting YOU and your loved ones from the silent menaces that plow the web and seek to harm you. Learn about internet surveillance, the best internet security and PC security from cyber security expert, Dr. Leland Benton. As a cyber security expert Dr. Benton performs internet

security reviews and cyber security consulting. Protect yourself today!

**Judgment Not Included $6.87**
**Kindle Version**
http://www.amazon.com/dp/B00CPRSQ3E
**PDF Version**
https://www.paypal.com/cgi-bin/webscr?cmd=_s-xclick&hosted_button_id=K9DCZTZ66Y9XL

Crime and Mental Health – Judgment Not Included is all about unbalanced people that commit heinous crimes. It discusses in detail crime and mental health, unbalanced, unbalanced people, mentally ill, mentally disturbed people, mental health issues, and mental disorders as they pertain to crimes committed by unbalanced people. Written by one of the nation's leading behavioral scientists, Dr. Leland Benton is the author of over two dozen self-help books and nonfiction behavioral science texts. He is a best-selling Amazon author with over 200-books published on Amazon alone. You need to read this book because it teaches you how to protect yourself from unbalanced people as well as why unbalanced people do the things they do. This intriguing book leaves no stone unturned regarding the current events such as the Boston Marathon bombing, the Aurora, Colorado theater shootings, Sandy Hook Elementary School shootings and more.

**Protecting Yourself from Cyber Crime $4.87**
**Kindle Version**
http://www.amazon.com/dp/B0095J3EIW
**PDF Version**

https://www.paypal.com/cgi-bin/webscr?cmd=_s-xclick&hosted_button_id=ANL4P777BCHNQ

Protect Yourself Online – Protecting Yourself From Cyber Crime is all about cyber security online and computer security online. This book shows how to protect yourself and business from online cyber criminals using online computer security programs. Protecting yourself from identity theft and demonstrating various identity protection services as well as credit fraud protection are two of the most common cyber crimes. Protecting Yourself From Cyber Crime is about staying one step ahead of the cyber criminals that are out to steal your life. It only takes one time for it to really hurt! Cyber crime is increasing exponentially and it isn't a matter of if your will be a target; it is simply a matter of when. But the hunted can become the hunter and fight back. There is an array of free protection software that is easy to install and use and all of the software does a fine job of protecting you and your loved ones. You owe it to yourself to read this book and implement what it teaches. Written by one of the nation's leading cyber forensics investigators and behavioral scientist, Dr. Leland Benton imparts his 31-year expertise to all of his readers. Protect yourself today!

**Sleeping with Guns $6.87**
**Kindle Version**
http://www.amazon.com/dp/B00CS1IBZU
**PDF Version**
https://www.paypal.com/cgi-bin/webscr?cmd=_s-xclick&hosted_button_id=VSZ6KH5YFNK5L

Personal Self Protection – Sleeping with Guns is an epic book that examines the art of self-protection in today's world by examining such topics as guns, guns and crime, guns freedom and terrorism, guns in the workplace, personal protection training, personal protection security, and personal self protection. It delves into touchy topics such as gun control and the mindset of fear. It examines a balanced approach to life where a person can actually enjoy a quality life while still maintaining vigilance against danger.

It provides a variety of alternative forms of protection other than physical weapons such as guns, knives, mace and more. Its main premise is that the human mind is the best defense against any danger or peril. Written by one of the nation's leading behavioral scientist, Dr. Leland Benton examines the science behind the need to protect oneself and loved ones. Dr. Benton is also Chief Forensics Investigator for ForensicsNation and is responsible for over 1100 arrests and conviction of all types of criminals. He is highly qualified to write this book and with over 200-books written on Amazon alone, he is a prolific writer and speaker. This book is a part of his Cyber Crime/Cyber Forensics series of books.

**Stealing You $2.99**
**Kindle Version**
http://www.amazon.com/dp/B00778TT6E
**PDF Version**
https://www.paypal.com/cgi-bin/webscr?cmd=_s-xclick&hosted_button_id=JRW27WXC4H35C

How to Stop Identity Theft – Stealing You not only offers ways to prevent identity theft, it also provides identity theft tips, identity theft resource center, and identity theft help. It also provides information on how to report identity theft correctly and timely. In other words, it is the best desktop compendium on identity theft protection. Everybody knows what identity theft is and there are a plethora of products available that protect against identity theft. But do you know why identity thieves commit this crime and what you do to make their job easier? Now you can crawl inside the heads of identity thieves and see just how vulnerable you are and exactly how you made their job so easy to steal YOU!

**SurvivalNations Catalog**
**Download for Free**
http://www.filefactory.com/f/d8ed9a936f3f812e

Are you prepared to survive any disaster or crisis? If the police came to your door and gave you 15-minutes to evacuate, what would you do? Where would you go? What would you take with you? You need SurvivalNations Catalog to answer these questions. We've compiled everything you need to survive in one easy catalog that is at your fingertips. Order SurvivalNations Catalog today!

**SurvivalNations – Surviving a Disease Pandemic $6.87**
**Kindle Version**
http://www.amazon.com/dp/B00BFFZCHU
**PDF Version**
https://www.paypal.com/cgi-bin/webscr?cmd=_s-xclick&hosted_button_id=FJGWFMUJSAENW

SurvivalNations – Surviving a Disease Pandemic is an epic book describing all aspects of an outbreak of a worldwide pandemic and how to protect yourself and loved ones. It is part of Dr. Leland Benton's "Survival Planning series" of books and it describes flu epidemics, what is swine flu, h1n1 virus, what is h1n1, flu outbreak, foodborne disease, and contagious diseases. It is a comprehensive desktop compendium and guidebook that describes everything you need to survive any pandemic.

**Survival/Survival Planning**

Be A Prepper
http://www.amazon.com/dp/B007IL5OE6

PrepperNations Blueprint
http://www.amazon.com/dp/B00ARBZNCW

Be Prepared to Survive
http://www.amazon.com/dp/B007KJ0ANQ

The Truth About Federal Anti-Hoarding Laws
http://www.amazon.com/dp/B007J4KH4O

**Surviving A Financial Crisis $2.99**
**Kindle Version**
http://www.amazon.com/dp/B007J1QH3C
**PDF Version**
https://www.paypal.com/cgi-bin/webscr?cmd=_s-xclick&hosted_button_id=KTVMQ93UHXDME

Survival Planning – Surviving A Financial Crisis is all about survival preparation, survival information, food for emergency preparedness, supplies for disaster, emergency supplies food, emergency disaster supplies, disaster preparedness kit, and earthquake kits. But more importantly, it is learning how to survive a financial crisis.

It is smart reading and a must read for all family members. It is smart because it is part of a series called "Be Prepared to Survive" and in this series we hope for the best but plan for the worst. Science tells us that only the strong survive. I'm telling you that only the best prepared will survive. Yes, the world economy sucks and it is tough out there but this book will set you on the right path to sound financial planning.

This book provides sound financial guidance even if financial disaster doesn't strike and this author believes it won't. But things will continue to get tougher for at least the next 4-years.

**Surviving YOU $2.99**
**Kindle Version**
http://www.amazon.com/dp/B007J3M6A8
**PDF Version**
https://www.paypal.com/cgi-bin/webscr?cmd=_s-xclick&hosted_button_id=AASNT9YREFQUA

Surviving You is all about leaving your own worst enemy behind – YOU – and becoming your own best friend. We all do things we shouldn't knowing full well that they are either harmful to us or simply plain wrong but we do them anyway. Now you can learn why you do the things you do but more importantly why you don't do the things you should.

The author – Dr. Harry Jay – is one of the leading behavioral scientists in the country and his style of writing makes it easy for you to better understand everything about yourself. But then he takes it a step further and shows you corrective protocols to improve your life. This is a must read book for your personal library.
Get a copy today and soon you will be Surviving YOU!

**The Mind Of a Con Man $6.87**
**Kindle Version**
http://www.amazon.com/dp/B00CO2BQHI
**PDF Version**
https://www.paypal.com/cgi-bin/webscr?cmd=_s-xclick&hosted_button_id=DRUCWHNYDP8F2

Manipulation – The Mind of a Con Man is a book you have ever read before but it is a book you should read! I am going to take you on an adventure into the human mind and show you not only why con men do what they do but why you do the things you do too. It is a unique book describing con man games, con man tricks, con man traits, con man terms, manipulation, emotional manipulator, deception & lies. It is an eye-opening expose taking you into the mind of con men and discovering why they do what they do. This book leaves no stone unturned as it delves deeply into the subject matter. It first describes the Type 1 con men, who are individuals who work hard at the deceptive profession but then it goes even further into Type 2 con men, which you come into contact daily through friends, family, co-workers ,etc that attempt to manipulate you into doing something. This book will fascinate you and you will see yourself within its pages as you learn all about deceptive people, the ways they operate, their tricks, their games and much more. Written by one of the nation's leading behavioral scientists, Dr. Leland Benton is the author of over two dozen self-help books and nonfiction behavioral science texts. He is a best-selling Amazon author with over 200-books published on Amazon alone. You need to read this book.

**The Power of Trained Observation $6.87**
**Kindle Version**
http://www.amazon.com/dp/B00BSRYMGW
**PDF Version**
https://www.paypal.com/cgi-bin/webscr?cmd=_s-xclick&hosted_button_id=QLVW8RH86YW42

Observation Training – The Power of Trained Observation is a series of online observation training courses designed to enhance your leadership skills training and general awareness. You look but you do not see EVERYTHING; you listen but you do not hear. "The Power of Trained Observation" teaches a person how to see EVERYTHING that the eye takes in and how to evaluate it in the conscious mind so the person misses nothing. Learn how the mind filters out stimuli and how to reprogram your filters to take advantage of everything you see and hear using the latest education information technology. Every sales and marketing executive should read this book and take advantage of this brain training online. This book is for anybody in business and investing, marketing and sales, and small business & entrepreneurship. The courses offered are the exact same online police training courses used to train law enforcement. When it comes to observation training, not only is this one of the only courses available, it is the best online training available. Written by one of the nation's leading behavioral scientists and instructors, best-selling author, Dr. Leland Benton is the author of over three dozen books dealing in a variety of behavioral science subjects. He is a best-selling Amazon author with over 200-books published on Amazon alone. If you have a desire to see and hear everything and not miss any opportunities then you need to read this book.

**Why Women Should Not Use Online Dating Services $2.99**
**Kindle Version**
http://www.amazon.com/dp/B006J9EMH8
**PDF Version**
https://www.paypal.com/cgi-bin/webscr?cmd=_s-xclick&hosted_button_id=23GNKD94XL6C2

Cyber Dating Dangers – Why Women Should Not Use Online Dating Sites demonstrates the online dating scams to unsuspecting online singles using singles sites. How online dating is dangerous is described in this book and should be used to understand and spot scam artists so a person can conduct safe online dating. It goes without saying that a person should be careful what online personals they post. Being a woman today is not easy and although the Internet has provided tremendous opportunities, it has also provided criminal elements the very same opportunities to practice their ugly trade. Women that use online dating sites need to read this book!!! You have been warned!

**ForensicsNation Catalog**
**Download for Free Here**
http://www.filefactory.com/f/d3eac5e74de46025

Have you been hacked online? Have you had your identity stolen? Have you been receiving weird emails? ForensicsNation Catalog provides you with all the tools to become an amateur sleuth. Be the hunter and not the prey! ForensicsNation Catalog is amateur forensics products enabling you to become an amateur internet sleuth. Cyber-Crime is increasing and now ForensicsNation offers the exact same products it uses to catch the bad guys. Now you can easily find anyone you want and conduct your own investigative searches using the forensic tools we offer.

www.ingramcontent.com/pod-product-compliance
Lightning Source LLC
Chambersburg PA
CBHW071000050326
40689CB00014B/3428